BYGONES

BYGONES

*Highlights From
Nottinghamshire's Past
Volume One*

First published in Great Britain in 2001 by
The Breedon Books Publishing Company Limited
Breedon House, 3 The Parker Centre, Derby, DE21 4SZ.

© Nottingham Evening Post, 2001

All Rights Reserved. No part of this publication may be reproduced, stored in a retrieval system, or transmitted in any form, or by any means, electronic, mechanical, photocopying, recording or otherwise without the prior permission in writing of the copyright holders, nor be otherwise circulated in any form or binding or cover other than in which it is published and without a similar condition being imposed on the subsequent publisher.

Bygones

Compiled by Andy Smart

Jacket designed by Rob Naylor

ISBN 1 85983 248 2

Printed and bound by Butler & Tanner, Frome, Somerset
Cover printing by GreenShires Ltd, Leicester

Contents

	Introduction	7
Chapter 1:	By Royal Appointment	8
Chapter 2:	When Coal was king	14
Chapter 3:	Nottingham's Century	20
Chapter 4:	Down the pub	29
Chapter 5:	Dial 999	33
Chapter 6:	Goose Fair	41
Chapter 7:	A time for heroes	49
Chapter 8:	Here is the weather	57
Chapter 9:	The Monocled Mutineer	62
Chapter 10:	Six of the best	65
Chapter 11:	The dancing years	71
Chapter 12:	Justice	76
Chapter 13:	Wembley wonders	83
Chapter 14:	The silver screen	89
Chapter 15:	Glorious Empire	101
Chapter 16:	Service with a smile	108
Chapter 17:	A fine designer	116
Chapter 18:	An actor's life	120
Chapter 19:	Lawrence and Sillitoe	126
Chapter 20:	General Hospital	132
Chapter 21:	Harold Larwood	139
Chapter 22:	Jesse Boot	145
Chapter 23:	Old Market Square	153
Chapter 24:	King Tommy	159
Chapter 25:	Cloughie's other half	162
Chapter 26:	Barefist fighters	170
Chapter 27:	Torpedo Tom	175
Chapter 28:	Your Evening Post	179

Acknowledgements

This volume has been compiled from articles which have appeared in the monthly Bygones supplement over the past four years and which involved the contribution of numerous journalists at the *Evening Post*, both past and present. Principal writers involved during that time include Jeremy Lewis, David McVay, John Brunton, Vicky Anning, Edward Jarvis, David Lowe, Andy Smart and Mark Patterson. Their work has been supplemented from the vast archives in the *Evening Post* library and the contributions of dozens of readers whose memories have been stirred by the different subjects we have chosen to reflect and without their letters, stories and photographs, Bygones could not have achieved the popularity and success it enjoys.

Introduction

IN March 1997, the *Evening Post* published the first of a new monthly magazine devoted to the increasingly popular subject of nostalgia.

Bygones was originally planned to run until the end of the year when its future would be reassessed. It was an instant success and now, more than 50 issues later, it is still going strong with no apparent lessening in demand for information about the past, memories of the way things used to be and a certain longing for a life which we will never see again.

Bygones travels the world. The subscriptions department of the *Evening Post* has regular orders for Bygones from Canada to Australia, America to South Africa. For ex-pats who have fond memories of Nottingham, it has proved to be an essential link with the 'old country'.

The popularity of the monthly series led to the *Evening Post* expanding its in-paper Bygones feature which now covers four pages each Monday as well as a nightly column of brief items culled from the headlines of yesteryear.

For some time it has been felt that articles included in the monthly supplement should be collected together in book form – hence this publication.

Because we are talking about more than four years of Bygones: hundreds of articles, millions of words, this collection is very much a selective... the Best of Bygones if you like.

It reflects the work of the many journalists at the *Post* who have worked on the series since it started, and also the contributions of members of the public who send in their articles, letters and personal photographs which help make Bygones such a favourite among our readers and so eagerly anticipated every month.

There is no reason why more publications should not follow. As long as the popularity of Bygones continues... as long as the people of Nottingham and Notts have memories, photographs, stories, anecdotes they want to share... so the monthly edition will continue and more features will be available to gather together in future collections.

So just relax and enjoy this journey back in time – and if it inspires you to write to us, we look forward to reading your comments.

Chapter One
By Royal Appointment

ON a bright morning in 1843, the Royal train steamed into Nottingham Midland Station and her Royal Highness Queen Victoria stepped down onto the platform to be greeted by various dignitaries including the Mayor and the county's Lord Lieutenant.

A military band played and soldiers formed a guard of honour for the Royal party which had arrived from Chesterfield after a stay at Chatsworth House.

The Queen and her entourage then made their way into the open air, clambered aboard their carriages and trotted off down a newly constructed highway en route for Belvoir Castle, home of the Duke of Rutland.

King George V and Queen Mary pictured in Woodthorpe Park where they were greeted by thousands of local people during their visit to Nottingham in 1928.

Edward Prince of Wales, later and briefly, to be crowned King Edward VIII, is welcomed to Nottingham for an official visit on a specially constructed stage in the Market Square. Readers of Bygones might well remember the occasion, and the date. Write to Bygones at the *Evening Post* if you have memories of this royal visit.

It is not recorded if the young Queen, she was 24 at the time, bothered to look out of her carriage window at the town, but if she did, it was the only sight of Nottingham she ever had.

For unlike her ancestors, or her descendants, Victoria never made an official visit to the town dubbed Queen of the Midlands.

The city fathers named that highway Queen's Road in her honour and erected a handsome statue to her memory but the citizens were never given a chance to gaze on the Royal personage. Strange that she did not follow in the footsteps of English monarchs from the time of Henry II, through to a couple of Richards and a John and on to Charles I, who all held Nottingham close to their hearts.

Fortunately, the 20th century monarchs made up for Victoria's absence.

In fact, it was in June 1914 that King George V and Queen Mary became the first reigning monarchs since Charles I to make an official visit.

The day was declared a bank holiday, thousands lined the processional way from Platform 5 of the Midland Station to The Forest, Wollaton Hall and the Market Place. Children from every school in the city gathered on The Forest to sing the National Anthem and the Royal party toured Lace Market factories including Birkins, Thomas Adams and I. and R. Morley.

George and Mary returned in 1928 to open new buildings funded by Sir Jesse Boot at the University of Nottingham, followed by a visit to the Royal Agricultural Show at Wollaton Park. As a mark of their love for the city, Queen Mary wore Nottingham Lace and in return city folk decorated every lamp post and every window with bunting, flags and flowers.

In July 1943, guarded by a security blanket because of the war, George VI and Elizabeth came to Nottingham to boost the morale of the workers on the home front.

King George VI and Queen Elizabeth pay a morale-boosting visit to Nottingham in 1943. Such visits were clouded in secrecy because of the war, but thousands of citizens managed to get wind of their arrival and packed the Old Market Square to greet them.

Top secret it might have been, but 3,000 people were there to greet them in the Market Square before they visited Chilwell Depot, Wilford power station and Boots.

It was a young Queen Elizabeth II who arrived in Nottingham on July 6 1955 to be greeted by five-year-old Angela Paget of Western Boulevard who presented a bouquet on The Forest.

Birkins was again chosen for a Royal visit during which the Queen provided a magic moment for machinist Rose Smedley of Broxtowe who had a brief chat with her.

Then the Queen, with the Duke of Edinburgh, indulged her love of horses by watching the showjumping at the Royal Show in Wollaton Park.

It would be 13 years before Queen Elizabeth returned to Nottingham – and it rained.

May 10 1968, the heavens opened. But 15,000 city schoolchildren still turned out to line the Royal route and the *Post* reported: "The radiance of her smile brightened the dullness of the weather."

The Queen was in the city to visit cycle manufacturers Raleigh, much to the delight of employees who saw the Royal party drive into the factory in an open top Land Rover.

Brian Jones recalled a narrow escape for the Queen who was standing up in the back of the Land Rover as it turned up the ramp to the Faraday Road bridge. She had to duck her head quickly to avoid the steel girders carrying the safety guard below the overhead conveyor.

"Raleigh did get the Queen's award for industry a few years later, so she couldn't have been too upset," Brian later told the *Post*.

Queen Elizabeth II is followed into the Council House by the Duke of Edinburgh for a civic banquet during her visit to celebrate her silver jubilee.

Jubilee year 1977, and the whole nation was celebrating with Queen Elizabeth on the 25th anniversary of her coronation.

Nottingham was certainly not going to be left out. Street parties burst into life throughout the city and on July 28 the Queen made her triumphal visit, dropping into Trent Bridge during the England-Australia Test and the QMC.

At one point the Royal party passed the end of Marcus Street, Castle Boulevard, where a party was in full swing, and a banner reading Welcome to Liz and Phil was clearly on show, much to the delight of organiser Janet Hemsley.

In the evening, an estimated 45,000 people lined Victoria Embankment for a Jubilee fireworks and water spectacular.

The following day an incredible crowd of around 250,000 people lined the road between Nottingham and Mansfield as the tireless Queen made her way to the north of the county.

In June 1990, the Queen brought her Royal smile to the inner city suburb of Hyson Green to dedicate a £3m building project at St Stephen's Church.

She had arrived at the Midland station where little Katie Pollard of Carlton got the honour of presenting the Royal posy and later, at St Stephen's, four-year-old Naomi McCalla of Sherwood handed the Queen a framed portrait of herself... with strict instructions to hang it in Buckingham Palace.

The Queen's most recent visit to Nottingham, to mark celebrations for the centenary of city status. In this magnificent photograph, taken in the Council House, she was pictured with 100 local people, one for every year of Nottingham's city life.

Then it was on to Fountaindale School and Portland Training College near Mansfield to present a number of awards with Falklands War hero Simon Weston among the recipients.

The Queen had one final date in Nottingham before the curtain fell on the 20th century – the highly significant celebrations to mark Nottingham's 100th year as a city.

The honour had been bestowed during the reign of one popular Queen and was now to be marked by another.

She made a county call first, in Mansfield, where 77-year-old Vera Quibley handed her a bunch of flowers. "She thanked me for the flowers. It was lovely," said a delighted Vera.

A visit to Queen Elizabeth School followed, the Queen being greeted by head teacher Nicola Atkin, and then by motorcade to Nottingham and a right Royal greeting in the Old Market Square.

After a walkabout, the Queen went into the Council House to see a model of Nottingham's proposed new Ice Arena, dedicating a silver marker which is now incorporated in the building and meeting sports stars including 12-year-old Charlotte Goodman of Cotgrave.

Her other duties included opening the new magistrates courts building and a visit to Boots in Beeston.

Throughout the 20th century, Nottingham has relished its Royal visits and welcomed Kings and Queens with a warmth and enthusiasm no other city could better.

They can be assured the welcome mat will still be out as the 21st century begins to unfold.

Chapter Two

When Coal Was King

IT was, and still is for a dwindling number, the hardest way to earn a living.

Hundreds of feet underground, hewing coal from the earth, miners put their health, their lives, at risk – day in day out.

For more than a century coal was king in Notts – now its reign is almost over and little remains of the once mighty coalfield that helped to power the nation and its Empire.

But coal gave Notts an identity and a character and a history that should never be forgotten.

Coal put bread on the kitchen tables, money in men's pockets. It inspired poets and authors, songwriters and film makers. It bred heroes and demanded sacrifices, and long after the last ton of coal has been turned, they will still tell stories about the pits of Notts.

The dawn of the 20th century saw coal mining reaching its peak.

Heading for the face.

A group of miners while away the time with a simple gambling game.

In Notts 32 collieries were turning out millions of tons a year. For every new pit that was sunk, a new village was born – rows of back-to-back colliery houses in the shadow of the headstocks and spoil tips which dominated the Notts skyline like black pyramids.

The county's industrial corridor stretched from Harworth in the far north through to Clifton and Wollaton in the south.

Twenty-four hours a day, the pit wheels turned the coal and a maze of railway lines carried it to the factories and power stations of the Midlands.

Most of the old pits, like Annesley and Babbington, Sutton and Teversal were sunk in the mid-1800s.

New pits followed before the Great War as coal production and demand soared.

Brookhill at Pinxton, Mansfield, Gedling and Welbeck, were all developed in the early 1900s.

Strikes and depression followed World War One, eroding the efficiency of the coalfield – and before recovery could be engineered, the country was plunged into new conflict.

The industry was ready for industrialisation when it came in 1947.

Miners, glad to see the back of the repressive colliery owners, welcomed it with open arms and within a few years, the Labour Government was investing large sums of money in modernising an industry which still relied on a pick and shovel as well as the honest sweat behind it.

Conditions underground improved out of all recognition with ventilation and safety measures top of the priority list.

Bath time... a typical scene in a miner's home in 1910.

But the switch also brought the first rush of closures as the government moved to merge small and uneconomical pits.

At the time, the men accepted the closure of pits like Watnall, Pinxton, South Normanton, Oakwood Grange, Lodge and Selston with little protest, but even if they could not see it, the industry had already begun to disintegrate.

Its demise began slowly in the late '50s, but would gather pace until it became a headlong rush.

The enemy was oil. As the market for coal shrank, so stockpiles built up. From 1957-63, collieries were closing at the rate of one a week on a national scale.

And even when the Tories were ousted by Harold Wilson, the industry freefall continued, the Notts coalfield losing Cotes Park, Radford/Wollaton, Cossall, Bestwood, Clifton, Kirkby Summit, Langton, Brookhill and Selston within the space of six years.

To the nation they weren't even names on a map but to the people who worked in the mines and lived in the communities around them, they were life itself.

And when the pits closed the heart of those communities stopped beating.

Miners toil away underground to hew coal from a deep seam.

When Kirkby Summit pit shut in 1968, the town also lost its railway sheds and its marshalling yards. There was virtually no alternative employment for hundreds of workers and the town teetered on the brink of catastrophe.

It was a situation that would repeated in mining villages the length and breadth of the country over the next 25 years.

Nothing could stop the decline, not the power of the NUM which brought down Ted Heath's government, not the support of a Labour government, not even a mini coal boom as oil prices rocketed.

The writing for the coal industry was on the wall and it would culminate in the last great industrial struggle of the 20th century, led by firebrand NUM leader Arthur Scargill.

His crusade was against pit closures, his enemy was Margaret Thatcher, his tactic was all-out strike. But he made a fatal mistake, refusing the option of a national ballot… and in Notts there were men not prepared to be dictated to.

Suddenly, the confrontation was deflected from a battle with a government to violence on the picket lines as Yorkshire's 'flying' pickets made dawn raids on Notts pits in a bid to bring working miners out and there they clashed with police in a series of ugly pitched battles.

The Notts miners were no more going to give into intimidation than they were to Scargill's dictate and on May Day 1984 they finally drove a giant wedge through the trade union movement when they broke away to form the Union of Democratic Mineworkers.

Scargill was defeated, a major power crisis was averted and, although it did not sit well with Notts miners, Prime Minister Thatcher hailed them as heroes.

But if they thought it was going to save the Notts coalfield, they were wrong. The closures continued. Even modern pits like Cotgrave could not survive.

Today, the few survivors are in private hands, fighting for a crust off the power generators' table.

Gedling Colliery's pit ponies ready for their annual two weeks holiday, pictured in 1960.

There is little community spirit left, a bare handful of workers when compared to the tens of thousands of men who dug the coal in the industry's heyday.

It is all a far cry from those summer days when miners would gather from around the country at Berry Hill in Mansfield for the annual NUM gala.

Leaders like George Cheshire, Len Clarke, Joe Whelan, Joe Gormley, Len Martin and Frank Haynes walked at the head of a proud procession, beneath the gaily coloured banners of each NUM branch.

Today, those banners lie out of sight in some welfare storeroom or office gathering dust, their colours fading.

A poignant symbol of a once great industry.

NUM officials on an inspection tour below the surface at Ollerton Colliery in 1974.

Nottingham's historic Elite Cinema building which opened in 1921.

Chapter Three

Nottingham's Century

TOWERING above Trinity Square with its restaurants, bars and multi-plex cinema, the Warner Entertainment Centre called The Cornerhouse is a powerful symbol of the new Nottingham.

It is a monument to the dawn of the new age, all neon and chrome, concrete and colour; an example of the pace of change sweeping through Nottingham as it ticks off the first few years of its second century as a city.

It took the place of the old *Evening Post* building, an edifice much mourned by some but which belonged to a different time. It was born of the Victorian era,

An early example of a Nottingham trolleybus – the service was introduced in 1927.

its buttresses and towers the indelible signature of architects who designed with the flourish of an artist.

It was there to welcome Nottingham's elevation to city status in 1897, an honour bestowed by the government of Lord Salisbury and approved by the old Queen in her jubilee year.

Nottingham's great men like General Booth, Jesse Boot and David Herbert Lawrence were around to see it happen and since that auspicious day, the city fathers have not sat back on their laurels.

We shouldn't be surprised at the progress Nottingham is making in the 21st century, we should be used to it.

The previous 100 years saw the city become an industrial giant, a pioneer of public health and housing, a seat of learning and a home to heroes.

It all began with a letter from Downing Street, signed by Prime Minister Lord Salisbury which read: "I have the honour to inform you that the Queen has been graciously pleased to direct that in commemoration of her Majesty's Diamond Jubilee the borough of Nottingham shall henceforth rank as a city.

"I have the honour to be sir, your obedient servant, Salisbury."

Nottingham certainly knew how to throw a party to celebrate, 46,000 people being ferried from every suburb to The Forest where breakfast was provided for everyone… at a cost of £600.

Virtually every house and shop throughout the city was decorated for the

Crowds line the Old Market Square for the official opening in 1929.

occasion with leading names like Hindleys, Goodliffes and T.H. Parr worthy of mention, Parr's window proudly proclaiming its loyalty to Victoria with the slogan: "A Queenly Woman. A Womanly Queen."

It lit the blue touchpaper for a century of change and achievement in Nottingham which can best be summed up in date order.

October 18 1897: The council took over the Nottingham Tramway Company and created Nottingham City Transport which continues to serve the people of Nottingham more than 100 years on.

February 28 1898: The Empire Palace of Varieties, with its ornate decorations and statues, opens its doors for the first time.

August 1 1898: The new Post Office in Queen Street is opened.

April 29 1899: Mundella Higher Grade School opens.

January 1 1901: The city's first electric tram route, Sherwood-Market Place, is opened, on the same day that Lady Bay Bridge was closed.

July 25 1901: Victoria Embankment opens

May 28 1903: The Midlands Industrial exhibition opens at Trent Bridge. A week later it is destroyed by fire.

January 15 1904: Midland Station opens.

April 22 1906: The First Albert Hall is gutted by fire. Three years later a new Albert Hall opened.

August 20 1907: Notts CCC win the County Cricket Championship.

November 9 1909: Jesse Boot is knighted.

A bevy of local beauties who took part in the Quincentenary celebrations of 1949.

March 24 1910: Nottingham's first purpose-built cinema, the Victoria Electric Palace opens in Milton Street.

December 6 1911: England beat the Australians five points to three in the first rugby international played in Nottingham – the venue was Meadow Lane.

May 12 1913: Suffragettes cause more trouble in the city, burning down the Nottingham Boat Club.

September 23 1916: Nottingham, which has sent thousands of men to war, is attacked by a Zeppelin which causes some bomb damage.

June 8 1917: The Victoria Cross is awarded posthumously to air ace Albert Ball.

August 22 1921: The Elite Cinema in Upper Parliament Street, is opened.

August 5 1922: Valley Road opens.

September 1 1924: The city purchases Wollaton Hall and park for £200,000.

April 24 1925: Nottingham's most popular dance hall, the Palais, opens.

May 4 1926: The General Strike begins.

April 10 1927: The first trolley bus runs on the Nottingham Road route to Basford.

October 6-8 1927: The last Goose Fair in the Old Market Square is held before its switch to the Forest.

May 22 1929: The Prince of Wales opens the new Exchange, otherwise the Council House.

July 31 1929: Notts CCC are again county cricket champions.

April 10 1933: More than 10,000 people welcome back Ashes hero Harold Larwood from Australia.

February 22 1935: Paul Robeson sings at the Albert Hall

September 6: 1936: The last tram runs from Daybrook Square to the Carter Gate depot.

August 4 1937: Tom Blower swims the English Channel in a record time of 13 hours 29 minutes and 24.1 seconds.

June 16 1938: New wholesale market in Sneinton opens.

October 16 1939: Carlton cinema (later the ABC) opens in Chapel Bar.

May 8/9 1941: The Nottingham blitz claims the lives of 169 people.

July 18 1946: The Sherwood Foresters and South Notts Hussars are granted Freedom of Entry to the city of Nottingham.

August 20 1948: The University of Nottingham receives its charter.

June 26 1949: Nottingham's Quincentenary Week starts, celebrating an historic charter granted to the city in 1449.

June 21 1958: The Empire theatre, for 60 years the venue which brought the biggest stars to Nottingham, hauled down the curtain for the final time.

May 2 1959: Nottingham Forest defeat Luton Town 2-1 at Wembley to lift the FA Cup.

December 11 1963: The new Nottingham Playhouse opens.

June 30 1966: Nottingham loses another familiar sight from its streets as the last trolleybus (No 522) completes its final run.

January 31 1968: BBC Radio Nottingham goes on air

March 1970: Paul Smith opens his first shop in the city.

January 6 1975: Brian Clough begins work as the new manager of Nottingham Forest.

September 25 1975: Radford-born Doug Scott climbs Mount Everest.

Nottingham Forest take an open top bus ride through the city after winning the European Cup for the first time.

April 22 1978: Forest win the First Division title for the only time in their history.

May 30 1979: Forest beat Malmo to win the European Cup and a year later retain the trophy with victory over Hamburg.

November 27 1982: Flamboyant Elton John performs live on the opening night of the Royal Concert Hall.

February 14 1984: To the familiar strains of Ravel's *Bolero* Jayne Torvill and Christopher Dean create skating history with a perfect score to win Olympic gold.

September 14 1987: Another county championship for Notts.

July 18 1991: The Showcase cinema gives *Robin Hood: Prince of Thieves* its UK premiere.

June 19 1995: The new and architecturally praised Inland Revenue building opens for business.

January 10 1996: Radio broadcaster Dennis McCarthy dies suddenly. Crowds line the streets to see his funeral cortège pass by.

May 1998: The *Evening Post* moves from Forman Street to its new home at Canal Wharf.

They are all historic moments in a city's life but, as *Post* Features Editor Jeremy Lewis wrote in the 1997 June edition of Bygones, it is the people that give it character.

Jayne Torvill and Christopher Dean perform their classic, gold-medal winning *Bolero* routine.

"In Nottingham's case a people who are sometimes slow to sing the city's praises, but quick to defend when provoked: a people ready to criticise when things aren't right – but criticise constructively; a friendly, relaxed, sensible people whose greatest strength is the ability, once they have questioned the need for change, to embrace it positively.

"We're in the mood for the second century."

Chapter Four
Down the Pub

Some say the art of brewing beer was a gift to the ancient Egyptians from Osiris, the god of agriculture – so let's raise a glass to the old boy and say cheers!

Because Nottingham has always had a fondness for a pint and a string of legendary breweries to supply the local thirst.

Sadly, most of the familiar names have gone, swallowed up the giants of the industry, and with them have gone some of our favourite city pubs.

Although the city's brewing history doesn't go back quite as far as the Egyptians, it is likely beer was being made in medieval times, using the cool caves for fermentation and storage, as visitors to Ye Olde Trip to Jerusalem or The Loggerheads will be able to experience for themselves.

Early taverns brewed their own ale for consumption on the premises. And as the industrial revolution brought high-density housing to Victorian Nottingham, 'cottage' breweries sprang up to service pubs within dray carting distance.

Long forgotten names from the past include the Alfreton Road Brewery, Thomas Loscoe Bradley at Basford, the Carrington Brewing Company, Dickens Hickton, the Dolphin, Wheatsheaf and Prince of Wales.

The old Nottingham Brewery, creator of Rock Ales and Maltanop, was to be

Two early views of the Royal Children.

The Salutation Inn.

The Flying Horse Hotel, one of Nottingham's most historic inns, which is now a shopping arcade.

found alongside the Filly and Firkin, Watson Fothergill's grand pub design in Mansfield Road.

As transport made travel and communication easier, the reputation of Nottingham's ales brought drinkers from many miles to take the 'waters'.

A certain James Shipstone realised production had to be put on a modern footing and he moved away from the concept of neighbourhood breweries by creating the Star Brewery in New Basford which was the biggest in the city until it was closed by Greenalls in 1990. But even today, old drinkers mourn the loss of the original pint of Shippos.

Other major players on the fringes of Nottingham were to include the Kimberley Brewery of Hardys and Hanson, Mansfield Brewery and Home Brewery, the latter two having become victims of the modern trend of acquisition and rationalisation.

John Robinson built Home Brewery on an old cricket ground at Daybrook and its Robin Hood logo became a familiar label in the city and beyond.

But today Home Brewery is just another page in history, along with the many pubs Nottingham has lost to redevelopment.

Names like the Corner Pin and its Clumber Street neighbour the Crystal Palace, an old Shippos haunt which found a new life as an amusement arcade.

The Milton's Head was a name that twice appeared in Parliament Street only to vanish again and a whole host of names went beneath the bulldozer as Nottingham moved towards the 21st century.

Names like the Bowling Green, Wilberforce Tavern, the Cromwell Inn have been flattened, the Flying Horse is nothing more than a name these days and even today, those with memories long enough, mourn the passing of the Black Boy Hotel.

Elegant and luxurious, a symbol of more refined times, it attracted the rich and the famous through its doors.

To this day, it's demise is held up as the single worst piece of urban vandalism a council has ever inflicted upon our city.

But some favourite watering holes have survived, with their names intact, through the centuries.

Indeed, argument has long rumbled on about which one is actually Nottingham's oldest. Ye Olde Trip To Jerusalem laid claim to the title although the Salutation and the Bell Inn put up powerful evidence to the contrary and, finally, experts decided the honour should go to the Bell whose origins are lost in the mists of time but certainly go back more than 500 years to the days when it was a refectory building attached to a monastery. Caves at the rear date to Anglo Saxon times and it is believe they were used by the monks to store their ale.

Whatever the truth, the Bell, Trip, Salutation and others like the Royal Children and Yates's Wine Lodge, are part of Nottingham's heritage and it would be a tragedy if they were ever lost like the Black Boy.

Chapter Five
Dial 999

THE number is instantly recognisable – dial 999 for emergency.

There can be few people who, at some point in their lives, have not needed to call up police, fire or ambulance to get them out of a scrape or come to the rescue of a friend, relative or even a complete stranger.

It is difficult to imagine our lives continuing as normal without the

A line up of city ambulances pictured in Shakespeare Street in 1964.

Ruddington St John Ambulance members with their ambulance pictured in 1943.

emergency services, ready and willing to come upon the dialling of three little numbers.

In the city of Nottingham that critical response to calls for help has been fairly instant for well over 100 years.

They may have had primitive beginnings but the services have grown with the times and always endeavoured to put the public first.

In the beginning, both the fire and ambulance services were actually manned by police officers. Constables manned first aid points around the city in the days when ambulances were little more than stretchers on wheels, making the journey to hospital something of a dubious form of salvation.

Fire engines were equally primitive. By 1837, Nottingham boasted six mainly old 18th century contraptions which did not get updated until 1864 when the city's first steam engine gave a public demonstration in the Great Market Place and three years later, the Watch Committee paid the princely sum of £650 for a state of the art Shand and Mason machine.

The city's Fire Brigade was up and running... although still with policemen at the helm.

For the county constabulary, newly formed in 1840, the tools of the trade – a truncheon, whistle and a fair degree of courage – remained constant as the force tried to combat poverty, drunkenness and neglect amidst the wretched slums and desperate lower orders that Victorian England and the Industrial Revolution helped to create.

Nottingham was shamed by the worst slums in the country and, inevitably, they spawned a criminal fraternity which needed some handling as local history books can confirm by the number of hangings that took place within the city limits.

The Nottingham Reform Act of 1835 was the first step towards introducing a modern system of policing.

The following year the new Nottingham Borough Police Force started to operate at a cost to the city of £734 4s 5d a year.

Officers were charged with the responsibility of "security of person and property, the preservation of public tranquillity and the prevention of crime."

A county force followed in 1840, necessary to cope with the flood of new workers to the county's mines.

It moved an early chief constable to remark that the increase in the number of thefts and robberies was due to "the great many strangers in the county."

The Nottingham Watch Committee ran the city police force, determined to prevent it falling under government control, and the early years saw a concentration of recruitment – always a thorny problem.

But while 13 boroughs and half the counties in the country could not muster a recognised police force, by 1874 Notts had 174 officers and at the turn of the century the figure was above 200.

Special constables were introduced during World War One and there 1,900 of these by 1918.

In 1968 the county and city forces combined to create the Notts Combined Police Authority – renamed Notts Constabulary in 1974.

As a result of the amalgamation, Shire Hall was found to be too cramped so

Nottingham was one of the first police forces to be equipped with walkie-talkies.

The city police introduced a new mobile police station for use at events like Goose Fair in 1961.

the headquarters were moved and in 1979, the £3m Sherwood Lodge establishment was opened.

Those are the facts, but they tell only part of the story for it is the men and women of the police force that give it character and identity.

Men like pioneering city chief constable Capt Athelstan Popkess, city centre legend Tug Wilson and tragic young officer Chris MacDonald who gave his life in the fight against crime more than 20 years ago, but is remembered to this day.

The Fire Service

It was after World War Two that the three emergency services took on separate identities with the local council assuming responsibility for fire fighting and in 1948 the newly-created National Health Service assumed control of the ambulance service.

Organised fire fighting in Nottingham can probably best be dated around 1864 when the first steam powered engine came into service.

That was followed three years later by a Shand and Mason costing £650 which was revealed to the public in a specially arranged trial in the Market Square.

There were gasps of admiration as a cascade of water towered 180 feet into the air and so impressed were the city fathers with their newly acquired machine, another was soon ordered to complement it.

1940s fire engines pictured in Shakespeare Street.

It was manned by fire fighters who came under the control of the local constabulary – but were never anything more than firemen. You wouldn't have seen any of them on the city beat.

The city brigade had its own team of electricians who installed Nottingham's first traffic lights and devised a street alarm system which involved pulling the emergency handle to light up a signal back at the Shakespeare Street HQ.

Earning around £3 a week, the firemen were housed in nearby accommodation in Shakespeare Villas or St Albans Terrace. They were on duty from 9am until 5pm every day and on call after 10pm.

According to local fire historian David Needham: "That 10pm curfew applied to everyone. You had to be at home in your firemen's lodgings. If you wanted to be out after 10pm for any reason, you needed permission from the police superintendent.

"You also had to get that, or at least some sort of blessing, to get married.

"The accommodation belonged to the police and they didn't want any dubious women living in there!

"There were giant bells upstairs and downstairs in the firemen's accommodation – as soon as they went off firemen were expected to be at their station on Shakespeare Street within a minute.

"If you had a sick child in the house and wanted it to sleep through the night you may have thought about turning the bell off or even muffling it with a sock.

"But then that was a disciplinary offence."

It was a tough regime, manned largely by ex-services personnel who obeyed, and rarely questioned, orders and discipline.

It was only later when recruitment spread to civilian trades that men began to question the way the service was run.

In fact, it was World War Two that totally transformed the fire service as the need for a more streamlined operation was exposed by the Luftwaffe's attempts to crush British resistance through their bombing campaign.

The service was brought under one body, answerable to the Home Secretary and then, on April 1 1948, the responsibility for fire fighting was taken on by local authorities.

The progress since then has been spectacular with more modern equipment and new or updated stations, plus an advance hi-tech nerve centre at Bestwood Lodge.

It is a far cry from the push and pull days of Victoria – but fire remains no less destructive, no less lethal; and the fire fighters' job still calls for a level of courage too often taken for granted.

The Ambulance Service

From the earliest ambulances which were little more than covered wagons pulled by horse to today's sophisticated vehicles packed with life-saving equipment and driven by paramedics skilled and qualified to help the sick and wounded, the ambulance service has come a long way.

Like so many other changes brought through the 20th century, war was to play a significant part in the development of the service.

During World War One, the Order of St John and the Red Cross joined forces to cope with the huge number of badly wounded soldiers coming home from the Western front.

So great was the number of casualties that hospitals like Nottingham City – then known as Bagthorpe Infirmary – laid tracks into the grounds to receive ambulance trains.

The City Hospital operated an early ambulance service for victims of disease and infection to be collected while Nottingham General became the major casualty hospital for the city, dealing with more than 400 accident victims in the year before World War One.

But a co-ordinated service for the civilian population was still some way off, although local collieries did run their own ambulances.

A major step forward came with the introduction of the Home Ambulance Service, originally run by St John and the Red Cross but, in the 1930s, gradually coming under the wing of local district councils.

During World War Two the Civil Defence organisation held joint responsibility, eventually making way for the National Health Service which arrived in 1948.

The first county ambulance officer was a man called Fred Jolley whose mammoth task it was to create from more than 30 separate, independent ambulance services at collieries, factories, councils and hospitals, a free ambulance service covering the whole of the county.

Setting up headquarters in West Bridgford, Mr Jolley began to sort things out and by June 1948 had 120 staff, 42 ambulances and 20 stations.

It was a remarkable achievement, borne out by these statistics: In the first five months of the service, 23,000 patients were transported by Notts ambulances covering a distance of 295,000 miles.

Fred Jolley went on to develop a service as good as any in the country. In fact, Notts was the first to introduce radio communications, a major advance in rapid response, and by the time he retired in 1974 the service boasted 52 ambulances, 280 personnel, an average of 285,000 patients a year and a mileage total in excess of 1.6m miles.

In 1974, the city and county ambulance services merged under the leadership of the city's chief officer, a hands-on leader by the name of Frank Wilkinson,

A demonstration of fire-fighting equipment pictured in 1968.

who became a familiar figure at accident scenes, arriving in his old red MG sports car.

Today, the service has expanded into a three county operation with Mike Handy, who took over from Frank Wilkinson in 1980, at its head.

He was the man in charge on that tragic night in January 1989 when a British Midland plane crashed on the M1 at Kegworth.

It was a night for heroes, with his officers performing remarkable feats of courage and determination to save dozens of lives.

It is a service we take for granted until we need them, but has proved its reliability time and time again over the years.

Chapter Six
Goose Fair

ROLL up, roll up! It's the greatest show of the year.

Nottingham's Goose Fair attracts thrill seekers in their thousands, wanting to experience a unique occasion when every fair operator in the land converges on The Forest with the highest, fastest, loudest and most colourful rides and side shows to be found.

It is Nottingham's pride – people from every walk of life cram onto the ever-expanding site each October to enjoy the sights and sounds, the tastes and smells of the greatest fair in England.

And, although the history books cannot pinpoint the date, that has probably been true from the day it started back in the middle ages when Nottingham was first establishing a reputation as a trading centre.

The theory is that it got the name of Goose Fair from the breeders selling their plump birds ready for the Christmas table.

Thousands of birds were driven from farms as far away as Lincolnshire, Cambridge and even Norfolk, their feet coated in tar and sand to avoid damage.

There are not many geese to be seen around the Forest these days but although the meaning might have disappeared long ago, the name has stuck and both event and title are now inseparable.

Setting up the stalls and rides always proved to be an attraction for local schoolchildren.

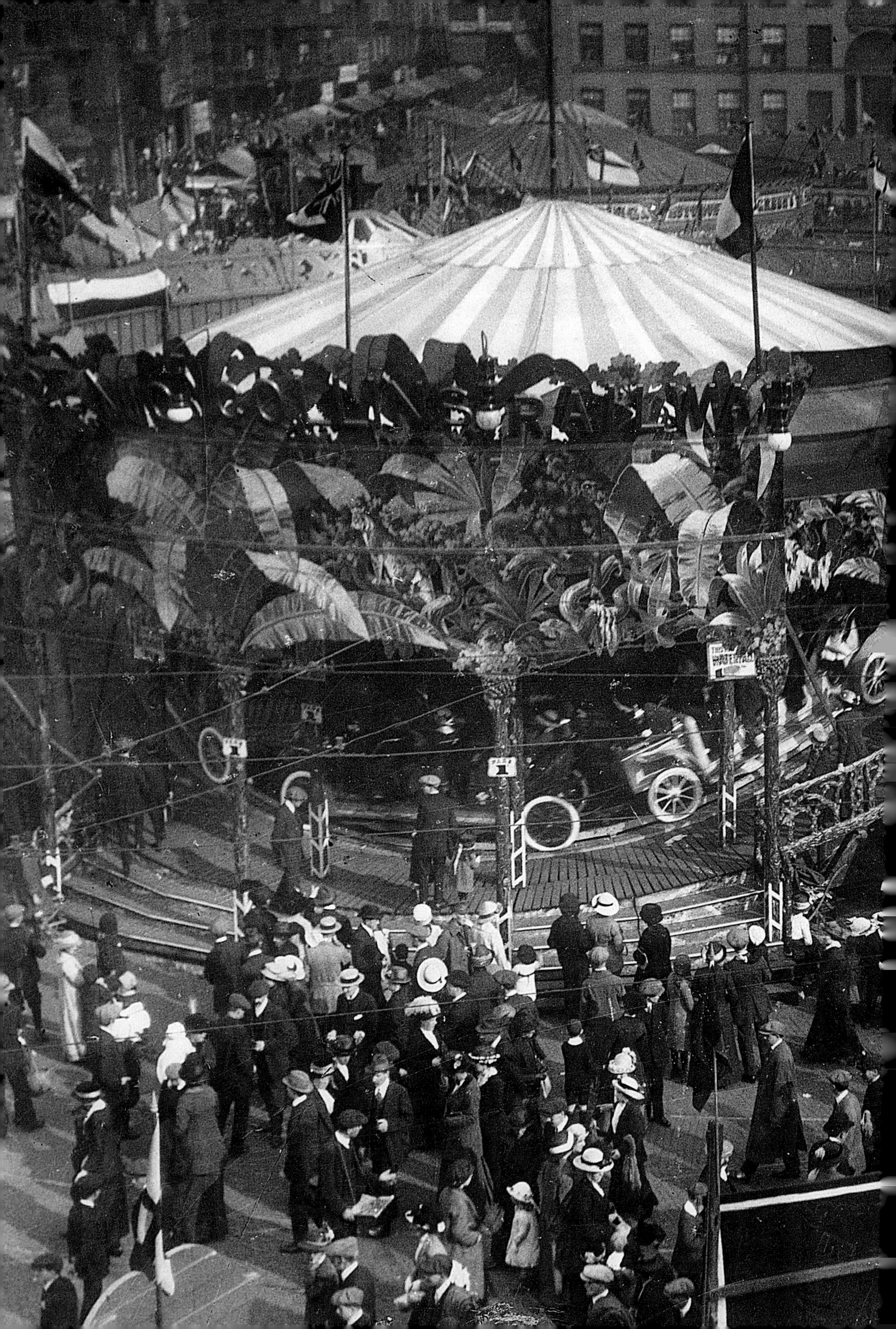

Goose fair in the days when it was held in the old market square before the Exchange building in the background was demolished to make way for the new Council House.

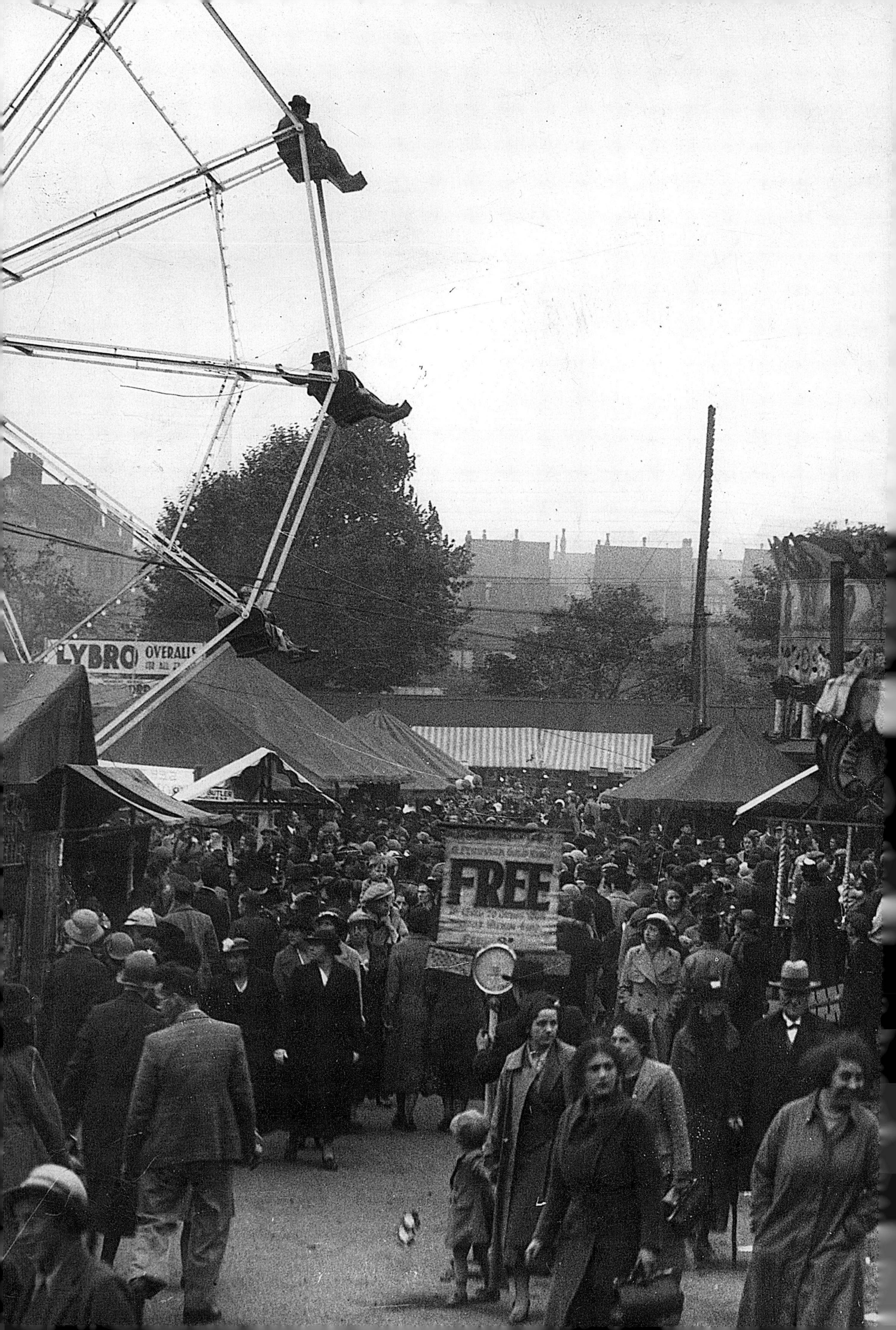
LYBRO OVERALLS
FREE

The Goose Fair in 1934, just five years after it had moved to its new home on The Forest.

According to the records, the first site of a Goose Fair is in 1542, but St Matthew's Fair was up and running in the 13th century – about 100 years after a rival event, approved by Henry II and sited at Lenton Priory.

For 300 years the Goose Fair had to play second fiddle to Lenton's extravaganza, at one time stretching over 12 days, which poured money into the coffers of the Church.

Agreements between the Priory-run event and Nottingham's fair were drawn up and repeatedly broken and somewhere along the road of history, perhaps in the 1600s, the Lenton fair disappeared from the local scene.

But nothing could stop Goose Fair, not even a riot.

That occurred in 1766 when the price of cheese rocketed.

A mob began hurling huge round cheeses down the slopes of Wheeler Gate and Peck Lane.

Distraught farmers could see their wares tumbling along in the dust and began chasing them, along with the town's mayor who was knocked flying by one of the cheeses.

Eventually, the 15th Dragoons were called out from the Castle to restore order – but the casualty toll included several injured and one man killed.

The Goose Fair was principally a centre for trade and remained so for around 500 years. Only performing artists like tumblers, jugglers and fire-eaters provided light relief. But in 1793 a new innovation caught the imagination of the public and laid the foundations for the fun and games that Goose Fair has come to represent.

A waxworks exhibition was set up in a fishmongers in Long Row. And soon after Madame Tussaud opened a travelling exhibition alongside the traders' stalls.

Animal shows became popular as William Howitt recorded in 1830. "Cages of wild beasts, theatricals, dwarfs, giants and other prodigies and wonders, all manner of wild and peculiar looking people, strollers, beggars, gypsies, singers, dancers, harp players, Indian jugglers… and similar wonderful artists."

Within living memory, Bostock and Wombwell's travelling show included bears, wolves, elephants and big cats.

They were transported around the country in a fleet of vehicles including two Burrell traction engines called Nero and Rajah, and a Robey tractor called Bengal.

Photographs show that the animals were not always kept in the best of surroundings and such an attraction could not be envisaged in these days of animal rights.

But satisfying public curiosity was the name of the game and the more exotic or unusual, the more likely it was to prove a sure-fire moneyspinner.

Where else could the poor people of Nottingham ever expect to see a caged lion, a pelican in the flesh or perhaps touch a real live elephant.

The crowds grew ever bigger, cramming the narrow streets around the Old Market Place, filling them with colour and noise and excitement.

Goose Fair became the most important date on the calendar – military service personnel even insisting on compulsory leave so they could join in the festivities.

It was somewhere you could buy anything from a cow to a rocking horse, see anything from a bearded lady to a five-footed sheep.

It survived despite complaints about the threat it posed to the moral well-being of the citizens, and their physical well-being after medical 'experts' claimed it was a "fruitful source" of infections and contagious diseases like smallpox, scarlet fever and measles.

In the early 1800s, the arrival of instruments of pleasure such as merry-go-rounds brought forth a declaration from the city fathers against those "disgraceful and dangerous machines called merry-go-rounds, instruments of folly and immodesty."

The biggest threat to Goose Fair, which led directly to its reduction from eight days to three, was the decline in trade.

Better communications meant people did not need to travel into Nottingham to stock up on goods and chattels.

As the commercial side declined, so did the duration of the fair and by 1880 it was down to three days.

Had it not been for the invention of steam, who knows what might have happened.

Steam brought a profusion of roundabouts and by the turn of the last century, Goose Fair had become, principally, an entertainment attraction.

And as invention and imagination broadened, so did the array of attractions: in came the helter skelter, big wheel, cakewalk and even an electric scenic railway.

Some rides, like the Ski Ride which saw pleasure-seekers pulled over snowy slopes by galloping horses, failed to catch on. The Skid lasted only a couple of years and in 1992 the once-popular Noah's Ark made its last appearance.

Any reflection on the history of Goose Fair would be incomplete without mentioning the boxing booths.

You could smell the aroma of freshly rubbed liniment emanating from Ron Taylor's splendid attraction – part of the Goose Fair scene for more than 60 years during the 20th century.

This photograph, from the collection of Douglas Whitworth, shows Union Jacks flying proudly over the scene of the first Goose Fair to be held after World War Two.

The Taylor family were there in the Market Place and carried on at The Forest, challenging all to follow in the footsteps of Bendigo and Ben Caunt, Nottingham's great bare knuckle heroes.

At one time or another legendary names such as Randolph Turpin, Tommy Farr and Freddie Mills all had spells with the Taylor booth.

On a Saturday, their courage fuelled by a few pints of Shippos, the young bucks would step forward, eager to impress their girlfriends. If the fight was a good one, the cap would be passed round and the booth boxer could be assured of a decent pay day.

In 1927 came perhaps the biggest change in the fair's 700-plus years history.

It was moved from the market place to make way for Slab Square and the new Council House.

It's home would now be The Forest, a much more appropriate site for what has become one of the East Midlands major outdoor attractions.

Down the centuries, only 11 fairs have been lost – to two world wars and the plague of 1646. It is England's most enduring fair, and judging by the popularity it continues to enjoy, there is every reason to suppose that Nottingham Goose Fair will be celebrating its own millennium... around the year 2294.

Chapter Seven
A Time for Heroes

THE Victoria Cross, a small Maltese cross fashioned from the iron of a Russian cannon captured during the Crimean War, is the supreme award for gallantry under fire for the British armed forces.

Nottinghamshire has not been short of heroes from Crimean VC winner Francis Wheatley to World War Two figures like Captain Robert St Vincent Sherbrooke.

There are too many stories to tell here.

For very different, but equally deserving reasons, three figures stand out in local history.

One is a surprise. Few people had heard of a 19th century soldier by the name of GONVILLE BROMHEAD until Michael Caine portrayed him in the classic action film *Zulu*. Fewer still realised that this dashing Victorian officer was a former Notts schoolboy, educated at the Magnus School in Newark before going on to serve gloriously with the British Army.

In January 1879, Lieutenant Gonville Bromhead was an officer with B Company 24th Regiment of Foot South Wales Borderers, stationed at a temporary hospital housed in a mission post on the banks of the Mizinyathi River in Natal Province.

Fuelled by political greed for land and wealth, the British Army was waging war on the Zulu nation led by King Cetawayo.

It had begun badly for the British. Led by the arrogant Lord Chelmsford who had totally under-estimated the fighting capability of the Zulus, the first expeditionary force had been split into two separate bodies.

On the morning of January 22, while Lord Chelmsford was several miles away enjoying breakfast and preparing for a good day's sport, 8,000 Zulus advanced on a poorly guarded British camp on the slopes of a mountain called Isandlwana.

What followed was the worst single day disaster in British military history as the native warriors, mostly armed with nothing more than spears and clubs, massacred 1,500 men of the most efficient and successful army the world had ever seen.

Now Cetawayo sent part of his victorious army against the small outpost of Rorke's Drift where fewer than 140 men, a quarter of them sick or wounded, had been ordered to "stand your ground".

Bromhead and a Royal Engineers officer by the name of John Chard, organised a most remarkable defence behind barricades of mealy bags and upturned wagons, to drive off repeated attacks through a day and a night from 4,000 Zulus until a relief column arrived.

A total of 11 VCs were won at Rorke's Drift, the most awards from a single action. Gonville Bromhead was one of them.

Albert Ball's medals, including on the left, his Victoria Cross.

Handsome Captain Albert Ball is the subject for the cover of a magazine produced during World War One.

Today, his medal is on show at the South Wales Borders' museum in Brecon, a dress uniform is on show in Newark Museum and his portrait still hangs at the Magnus School where, for many years, the very mention of his name would result in a chorus of cheers.

While the local links with VC winner Bromhead were hardly known, the story of ALBERT BALL has continued to fascinate people since World War One.

If they were making a movie of his story, they would have to hire someone like Tom Cruise or Brad Pitt to portray a man who was like a pop star in his day.

Albert Ball was young, handsome and as brave as a lion.

At a time when war was depressing, the death toll a continuing blow to morale at home and at the front, the exploits of Albert Ball were a source of inspiration and hope.

The son of a wealthy Nottingham businessman, Albert Ball had been educated at Nottingham High School and then Trent College where he was a prominent member of the Officer Training Unit.

When war broke out in 1914, he joined the local Sherwood Foresters regiment but, fascinated by flight, he quickly transferred to the newly created Royal Flying Corps.

Ball proved to be a natural and daring pilot, a true warrior of the skies.

During his brief career, he downed more than 40 German planes, often

The GREAT·WAR

THE STANDARD HISTORY OF THE ALL-EUROPE CONFLICT
Edited by H·W·Wilson, author of
"With the Flag to Pretoria," "Japan's Fight for Freedom", etc.

Captain Albert Ball, D.S.O., M.C.,
Notts and Derby Regt. and R.F.C. Won the D.S.O. for successfully attacking six enemy machines in one flight.

Vol. VIII.]

July 22 1917: King George V presents Sir Albert and Lady Ball with their son's posthumous Victoria Cross.

tackling four or five enemy aircraft single-handed.

It is said he would land a bullet-ridden aircraft, jump out and climb straight into another to get back into action.

In his early months at the Front, Albert Ball would write home to his parents about the camaraderie and thrills of action, but in his later letters, shortly before his death, he had clearly become disillusioned and even said that at times he felt like a murderer.

The authorities were keen to bring him home and make the most of his national adulation on recruitment and war bond drives.

Tragically, he died on what was intended to be his final mission. He led his squadron into battle against planes from Baron Manfred von Richtofen's circus and during a dogfight was seen to chase a German plane into a cloud bank.

What happened next is forever shrouded in mystery but the result was a crash, in a field near the French village of Annoeullin, in which Ball suffered fatal injuries, dying in the arms of a young French woman who had rushed to his aid.

The German forces, recognising the hero who had lost his life that day, afforded him a funeral with full military honours.

It was a devastating blow for the nation, a heartbreaking loss for his parents.

His father, Sir Albert Ball, paid for a monument to be erected on the spot where his son died. A statue, paid for by public subscription, was erected later in the grounds of Nottingham Castle and every year a small, poignant memorial service is held there. The Castle Museum holds several touching mementoes as well as his medals – the Victoria Cross, a Distinguished Service Order with two bars, making him the first man in the history of the British

The Albert Ball statue in the grounds of Nottingham Castle.

Grenadier Guardsman Harry Nicholls, pictured right, with a wartime comrade.

Army to be awarded a triple DSO; Military Cross, the French Legion d'Honneur, and from the American Aero Club a diploma and medal. Ball was the first British aviator to receive that particular honour.

Albert Ball is also a hero still in the village of Annoeullin where is he is buried, and in the year 2000, the children there chose to honour the great English pilot by naming their new school in his honour.

The story of HARRY NICHOLLS is one of the most extraordinary in the 150 year history of the Victoria Cross.

Harry Nicholls was born into a large Meadows family in 1918 and got his schooling at Bosworth Road.

In later years, Harry Nicholls tried to make a new life in Rhodesia and is pictured, second right, on parade in Salisbury for a visit of King George VI.

His working life was unspectacular, but in the sports arena Harry was outstanding. He was a good footballer and a strong swimmer but really found his talent inside the square ring after learning the noble art at the YMCA club in London Road.

Possessing a strong sense of adventure, Harry decided to enlist in the army in 1936, at the age of 18, and his height automatically got him a place in the Grenadier Guards which has always had a strong link with Nottingham.

It gave Harry the chance to develop boxing skills which would see him crowned British Army heavyweight champion in 1938.

How much further Harry could have taken it we will never know – suddenly there was a bigger fight on his hands as the Grenadiers were sent with the British Expeditionary Force to France following the outbreak of war.

As Hitler's Panzers pushed west in its now legendary Blitzkreig, Harry and his comrades found themselves fighting on the banks of the River Escourt in Belgium on May 21 1940.

Harry's citation for the VC tells what happened next:

"Lance Corporal Nicholls was commanding a section in the right forward platoon of his company when the company was ordered to counter attack. At the very start of the advance he was wounded in the arm by shrapnel but continued to lead his section forward. As the company came over a small ridge the enemy opened heavy machine-gun fire at close range. Lance-Corporal Nicholls, realising the danger to the company, immediately seized a Bren gun and dashed forward towards the machine-guns firing from the hip. He succeeded in silencing first one machine gun and then two others, in spite of being again severely wounded.

"L.Cpl Nicholls then engaged the German infantry massed behind causing many casualties and continued to fire until he had no more ammunition left. He was wounded at least four times in all, but absolutely refused to give in. He has since been reported killed."

His wife Connie, mourning the loss of her husband, travelled to Buckingham Palace in the August of 1940 to collect his VC from King George V.

But, incredibly, Harry was in fact still alive and a prisoner of war, having survived his wounds thanks to the skill of German military surgeons.

When the news came out, Mrs Nicholls had to return the medal until her husband could come home, in 1945, and collect it himself, one of the rare occasions when a VC has been presented twice.

Life after the war was tough for Harry. The affects of his wounds blighted his life, his first marriage ended and finally he fell on hard times, spending his last days in a Grenadier Guards Association flat in Leeds where he died, in 1975. He is buried Wilford Hill Cemetery.

Chapter Eight
Here is the Weather

JANUARY 27 1947 – one of the worst winter days on record in Nottingham… and it was only just beginning.

Ahead lay an unprecedented number of consecutive days when the temperature would be below freezing, snow would lie up to two feet in depth and chaos and pain would be the order of the day.

For a country emerging from the ravages of war, it was hardly a recipe for optimism.

January opened with six degrees of frost and power cuts in West Bridgford as the Central Electricity Board endeavoured to conserve supplies.

A spokesman came up with the startling statistic that it would take 436 telephone calls to implement a power cut order.

But this was only the phoney winter – the real one began on January 27 when the mercury fell to 29F and four inches of snow fell on Nottingham.

March 1947 and residents of Bulwell are forced to adopt alternative methods of transport after the River Leen burst its banks.

Launching a boat during the floods in Dunkirk.

Transport immediately ran into trouble, a flu epidemic hit the population and schools were closed because of heating problems. And just to compound the misery, there was a shortage of lead for plumbers trying to tackle the first rash of burst pipes.

On February 3, the city water department handled more than 490 calls for help, including flooding at the Midland Bank on Milton Street. More than 5,000 Raleigh workers were sent home.

On February 4 there was more snow to test the patience and endurance of 300 corporation workers manning 50 lorries and six snow ploughs – it was their job to keep city roads open.

The *Post* weather expert commented somewhat ironically: "The outlook is nothing too encouraging."

Well, he got that one right. February 5, a foot of snow falls in Mansfield, in Lincolnshire its up to the top of telegraph poles and in Derbyshire, some of Hitler's miserable Wehrmacht are marched out of the POW camps to start road clearing.

On February 7 the *Post* reported eight inches of snow – and the closure of five north Notts collieries.

That contributed towards a growing fuel crisis, forcing Labour prime minister Clement Atlee to appeal to the country to save energy.

People in Nottingham, criticised for not showing 'that Dunkirk' spirit, were particularly alarmed about the shortage of fish and chips!

A patient arrives at the Holmewood Nursing home in Musters Road, West Bridgford.

Meanwhile in Stapleford four housewives were in court.. for sending their children out to steal coal.

February 19 was a record breaker – the 32nd night of frost, passing the mark set in 1917.

Two days later the *Post* had converted that to 269 hours of continuous frost and then tried this cheery piece of optimism: "At least we are at the end of winter and not the beginning."

The sentiment was lost on people struggling to work using planks for snow shoes, or the soldiers attempting to clear eight foot drifts in freezing temperatures as the wind howled round their ears on Mapperley Plains.

On the 24th, it was down to -29, coldest night of the century, and by the 27th a record 38 inches of snow had fallen since the dawn of the year.

And it got worse.

After a mini-thaw which was over almost before it had begun, a fresh blizzard dumped another 14 inches of snow across the county. Scores of people were taken to hospital with broken bones due to falls, a trolley bus crashed on Carlton Hill, villages south of the river were cut off by ten foot drifts and, once again, the luckless Germans had to leave the warmth of their barracks and help a nation brought to its knees in a way Hitler could never achieve.

By the time the big freeze had ended, the records would stack up like this:

*Nearly 320 hours of continuous frost.
*More than 600 out of 672 hours below freezing,
*Nearly 40 days of snow on the ground, up to 21 inches in depth.

But it had to end sometime. On March 8, the temperature soared to a balmy 42 degrees... and Nottingham was hit by the heaviest rainfall for 58 years. Out went the big freeze and in came the big flood.

If 1947 is remembered for the worst that winter could throw at us, few will forget the summer of '76 when the country sweltered through the most prolonged drought for 250 years.

There was no talk of the greenhouse effect or global warming, just a nation trying to cope with day after day of cloudless blue skies and a burning sun nudging up to the 90s.

It was the sunniest July on record with more than 250 hours of blazing hot weather and like everything else, there reached a point when everyone agreed you could have too much of a good thing.

It was caused by a large, stationary anticyclone which settled over the British Isles in June and just sat there bringing record temperatures, record low rainfall, hosepipe bans and forest fires.

The hosepipe ban for washing cars and watering gardens came in at the end of May when the government issued its Drought Order.

There was a general appeal for people to keep calm, conserve water and wait for the impending rain... and wait... and wait.

The heat got under everyone's skin. In Nottingham Shire Hall Mr Justice Bristow took the unprecedented step of allowing jurors to remove their jackets and barristers their wigs, during a murder trial.

Then came a timely warning from the British Medical Association about the dangers of sunbathing. Everyone knows about the links with skin cancer today, but it was not such common knowledge more than 20 years ago. A BMA spokesman said: "You do have some people who have no sense at all. They still sit out and fry."

As they burned, so did the undergrowth across large tracts of Forestry Commission land in the north of the county.

Fires raged in Sherwood Forest – not just as a result of nature – and Notts firecrews were facing the most demanding period in memory, answering more than 150 emergency calls a day as tinderbox dry grass and undergrowth burst into flames from a discarded cigarette or a shard of broken glass.

As June moved into July, temperatures hit 87.5F and an uncomfortable 63.3 during the night.

People were consuming water at dangerously high levels, drinking supplies dry. In a bid to cut back consumption, thousands of leaflets and car stickers were issued.

In Derbyshire, gritting lorries were brought out of summer hibernation to sprinkle a mixture of sand and grit on roads where tar was melting.

The *Post* conducted a readers survey to find some predictions for a hotter, sunnier future. "Heavy, turgid foods would go... it would be the death of Yorkshire puddings," said one. "The streets will be full of snoring dogs, like Portugal," said a well-travelled passer-by.

But the reporter especially liked the saucy keep-cool hint from one local lass who said: "I would keep my knickers in the fridge. What was good enough for Marilyn Monroe is good enough for me!"

There was a brief respite for two weeks during July before August burned its way onto the calendar, forcing the government to call an emergency cabinet meeting and appoint the nation's first Minister for Drought – ex-soccer referee Denis Howell.

In Nottingham, the weather took its toll. Baked sports grounds were closed, homes were hit by subsidence, burst pipes and leaking taps.

The hot, dry spell finally broke (perhaps Denis did a rain dance) and the rains came in September, although the Drought Order would not be officially lifted until October.

It came as a relief, but with winter fast approaching, most people were wishing for its return. Not everyone though. One reader sent in a letter which contained this Victor Meldrew style sentiment: "I loathe summer anyway. It only brings out the insects, sneering, transistor radios, and fat behinds in shorts!"

Fighting a brush fire during the drought of 1976.

Chapter Nine
The Monocled Mutineer

THE Government, particularly the War Office, breathed a collective sigh of relief when Percy Toplis, the rebel soldier from the pit village of Blackwell on the Notts/Derbys border, died in a police ambush in 1920.

Toplis had become a thorn in the side of authority ever since the day he stood before a court when he was just 11 years old.

That was in 1908 when he was found guilty of conning a Sutton-in-Ashfield clothier named Albert Levitt.

His punishment was six lashes of the birch, administered while he was strapped to a wooden table in the cells, and was meant to be a lesson that would return him to the straight and narrow.

But for young Percy Toplis, who came from an impoverished Derbyshire family, the die was already cast.

He was an opportunist conman with a violent streak who revered the exploits of Charles Peace, an infamous villain of the 19th century whose life ended on the gallows.

Even at that early age, Percy was warned by John Bailey, his head teacher at South Normanton Elementary School, that a similar fate awaited him after he was caught stealing collection money intended for a Christmas concert. That was Percy's last day at school.

By the age of 15, he was serving two years hard labour in Lincoln prison for forcing his attentions on a young lady – the second jail sentence of his young life.

But it was the outbreak of war that would eventually transform the teenage crook into public enemy number one.

Percy Toplis enlisted in the Royal Army Medical Corps and his first duty as a stretcher-bearer was at Loos during the Battle of Arras.

Amidst the snow, sleet, hail and mud, he saw 15,000 casualties shot, bombed and gassed. Toplis was not impressed. Desertion was already part of his game plan.

On his first leave, he obtained an officer's uniform, complete with the ribbon of the Distinguished Conduct Medal and returned to a hero's welcome in Blackwell. He also became a well known figure in London society.

Posing as a well-heeled officer and affecting a polished gold monocle to complete the dashing image, the handsome Toplis charmed the ladies and fooled everyone into believing he was from a much higher station in life than a lowly pit village in the Midlands.

He was eventually sent back to France, but immediately fled the fighting and joined a ragtag army of deserters living rough while the war raged around them

Disaffection was endemic. The endless slaughter of battle, the dreadful conditions of mud and disease in the trenches and the brutal treatment meted out on an infamous training ground at Etaples, known as the Bullring, festered along the front line and finally erupted in mutiny, days before Field Marshal Haig's Passchendaele Offence was due to begin.

Thousands of soldiers had to be withdrawn by the High Command to quell the uprising, briefly threatening the while campaign.

Percy Toplis, the monocled mutineer.

And Toplis was there, at the centre of the rebellion, leading a mob of about 1,000 rioting soldiers.

He confronted senior officers, forcing them to accede to the demands of the rank and file, and reducing humiliated Etaples commandant Brigadier General Andrew Thompson to tears.

A veil of secrecy fell across the while sorry affair – which included the massacre of Chinese and Egyptian dock workers who downed tools in Boulogne harbour, and the summary execution of dozens of deserters.

That was until the publication of The Monocled Mutineer by William Allison and John Fairley, a sensational book which eventually led to an acclaimed TV drama in which actor Paul McGann played Toplis.

However, we will have to wait a few years yet to learn what the official records say about the mutiny… the 100 years secrecy rule does not expire until 2017.

When the mutiny was finally quelled, Toplis went on the run.

He joined a bizarre underground society made up of deserters called The Sanctuary, who lived by stealing from troops and organising black market rackets.

Toplis was eventually captured in a French village and taken to a British military stockade under sentence of death.

But in the middle of the night, the resourceful mutineer dug his way to freedom, burrowing beneath the barbed wire fence, and ran for his life as guards' bullets whistled round his head.

Toplis' charmed life held true. He escaped, made his way back to England and finally arrived in Nottingham where he was able to celebrate Armistice Day November 11 1918, from the safety of his room at the Flying Horse Inn.

Nottingham must have seemed a dull and disappointing bolthole to the adventurous Toplis. War time austerity still gripped the city. Pubs were shut because they had no beer, street lights were still dimmed by anti-Zeppelin covers and after four years of grim news about slaughter on the Western Front, the population's celebrations of peace were somewhat muted.

The *Evening Post* reported: "There were none of the orgies associated with the relief of Mafeking."

Percy Toplis thought he was now immune from military justice and reverted to a life of crime, serving another six month jail sentence, before rejoining the forces with the Royal Army Service Corps.

But this was not out of some sense of loyalty to King and Country. Toplis had already showed that his loyalty was to himself.

No, the cunning Toplis had spotted another chance to make some money without having to work for it... a black market scam to relieve the Army of valuable stores.

He was always one step ahead of the authorities and when it looked as if arrest was imminent, he stole a car, drove out of his army camp and went on the he run again.

But like almost every desperate villain before or since, Percy Toplis' days were numbered. The net was closing in around him.

The final chapter in this amazing story began with the murder of a taxi driver named Sidney Spicer in Hampshire. Toplis was accused of the heinous crime and a manhunt was launched that would range from London to Wales, home to Derbyshire and Notts, and as far as Scotland before its violent end.

On a warm and pleasant June afternoon in 1920, Toplis was spotted walking along the Penrith road in Cumberland by a police sergeant who raised the alarm.

Armed officers rushed to the area and a trap was laid for the unsuspecting villain to walk straight into.

In the village of Plumpton Toplis was confronted by the police and shots rang out. When the smoke of gunfire had cleared, Toplis lay dead on the ground.

The incident, and Toplis' remarkable life story, made headlines around the nation.

The *Evening Post*, after official identification of the body by Toplis' sister who travelled north from Alfreton, ran the news beneath headlines that read: "Toplis identified – all doubts removed. Exit Toplis. End of Derbyshire soldier's career of crime."

The killing of such a notorious figure came as something of a relief to the authorities and although some journalists questioned the circumstances of his death – it was even raised in the House of Commons – a jury exonerated the police officers involved.

Toplis was buried in a pauper's grave overlooking Ullswater, marked only by the words "Shot dead by police in Plumpton".

It was many years later that friends raised the money erect a headstone on the spot, bearing the epitaph: In Grateful Memory of Percy Toplis, the Monocled Mutineer.

Chapter Ten
Six of the Best

ALTHOUGH it is a mere 33 years ago, the black and white film of the great event is now grainy and dated, the commentator's BBC voice adding to the feeling of a Bygone age.

Yet the feat performed that day beneath gunmetal grey skies in Swansea transcends eras. It ranks alongside all the great sporting feats… and to be honest, we are still waiting for someone to come along and match the accomplishment.

It belonged to the splendidly named Sir Garfield St Aubrun Sobers, it occurred on August 31 1968 – and anyone who was there, or saw it re-enacted on television will never forget it.

Sobers was the world's greatest all-rounder, a player who batted his way to a career total of 28,315 runs, bowled out 1,043 victims in a variety of different styles from pace to spin, and also took a remarkable 109 catches at Test level.

I once watched Gary Sobers playing golf in a pro-am with the man who was take over his mantle as number one all-rounder Ian Botham.

It was a revealing afternoon which said much about the man, always playing within himself, with a smile on his face and with a politeness not all sportsmen and women can claim. But one incident summed up the consummate professional.

It was a wet day and Sobers was bunkered on the far side of the green so he took his sand wedge and his putter to save having to make the walk back to his bag. But he didn't lay his putter on the wet ground while he made his bunker shot, he rested it on a tee to ensure the grip remained dry. Now there's attention to detail.

There was nothing quite so subtle about his approach to the bowling of Glamorgan's Malcolm Nash on that August afternoon in 1968.

Notts were in a commanding position at 308-5 thanks to solid contributions from Brian Bolus, Bob White and Graham Frost when Sobers walked out to the crease.

He had already decided to go for quick runs as the pitch was showing distinct signs of wear and 40 runs were notched up in next to no time.

But it wasn't enough for Sobers who had worked out that the short boundary on the Gorse Lane side of the ground was well within his range.

As Nash prepared to deliver the first ball of another over, Sobers took another quick glance and knew exactly what he was going to do.

"I made my mind up to hit the ball over it, irrespective where it was pitched," he said later.

"My intention was to swing so hard at each ball that even a mis-hit would clear the rope."

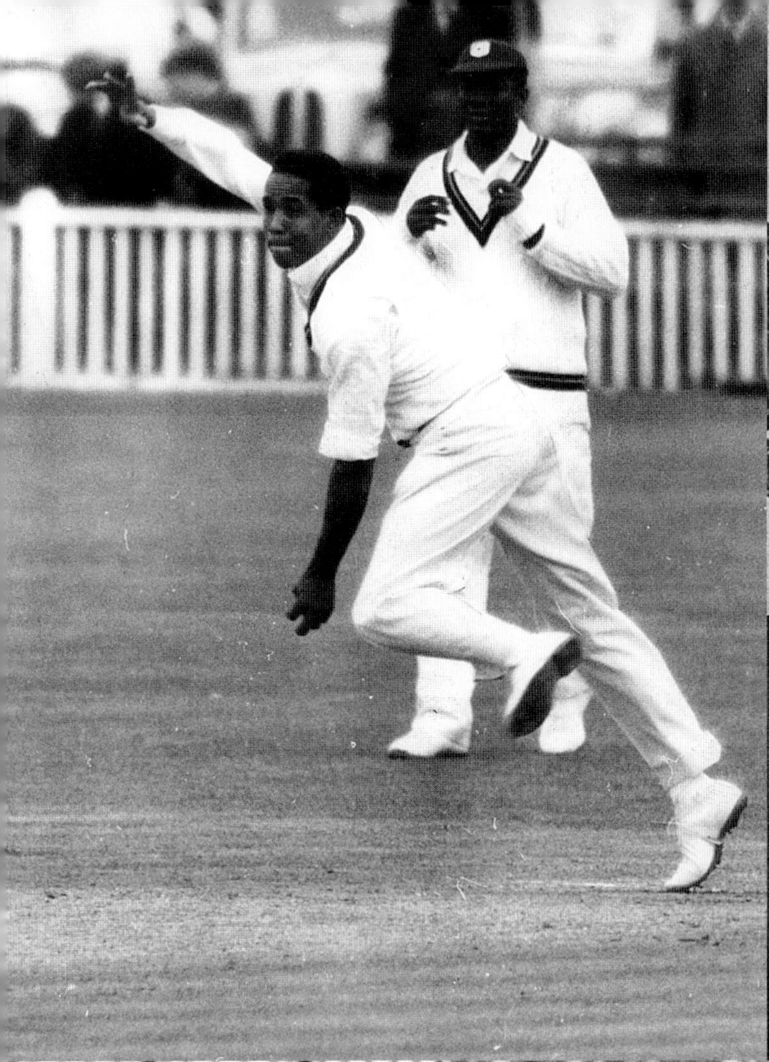
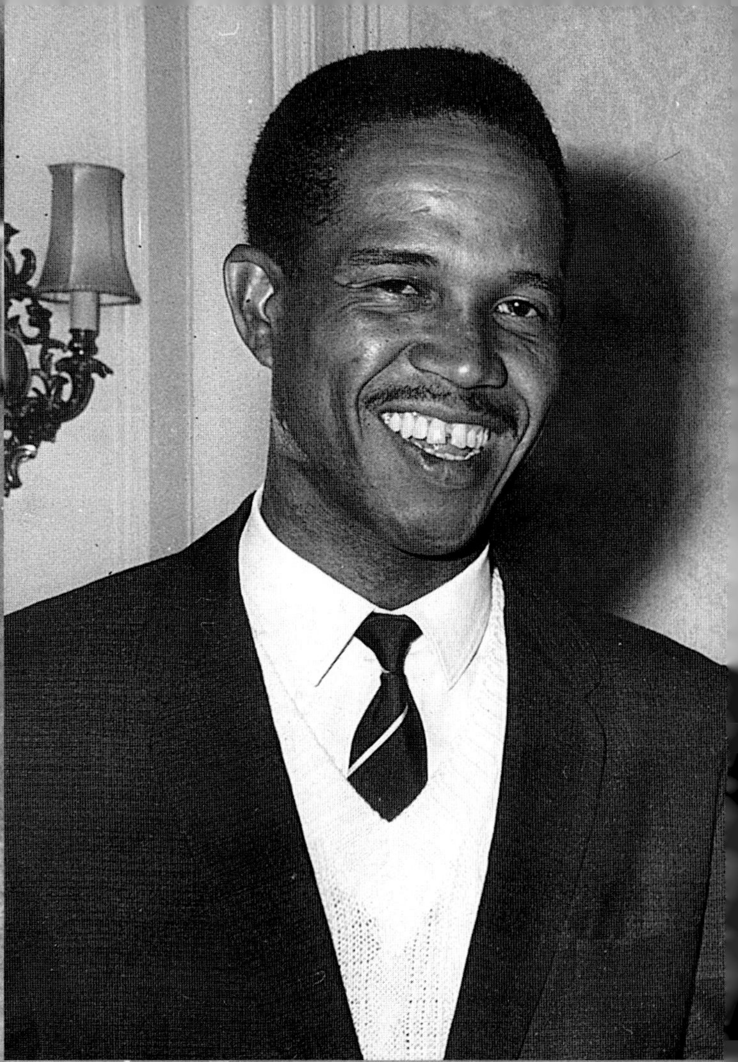
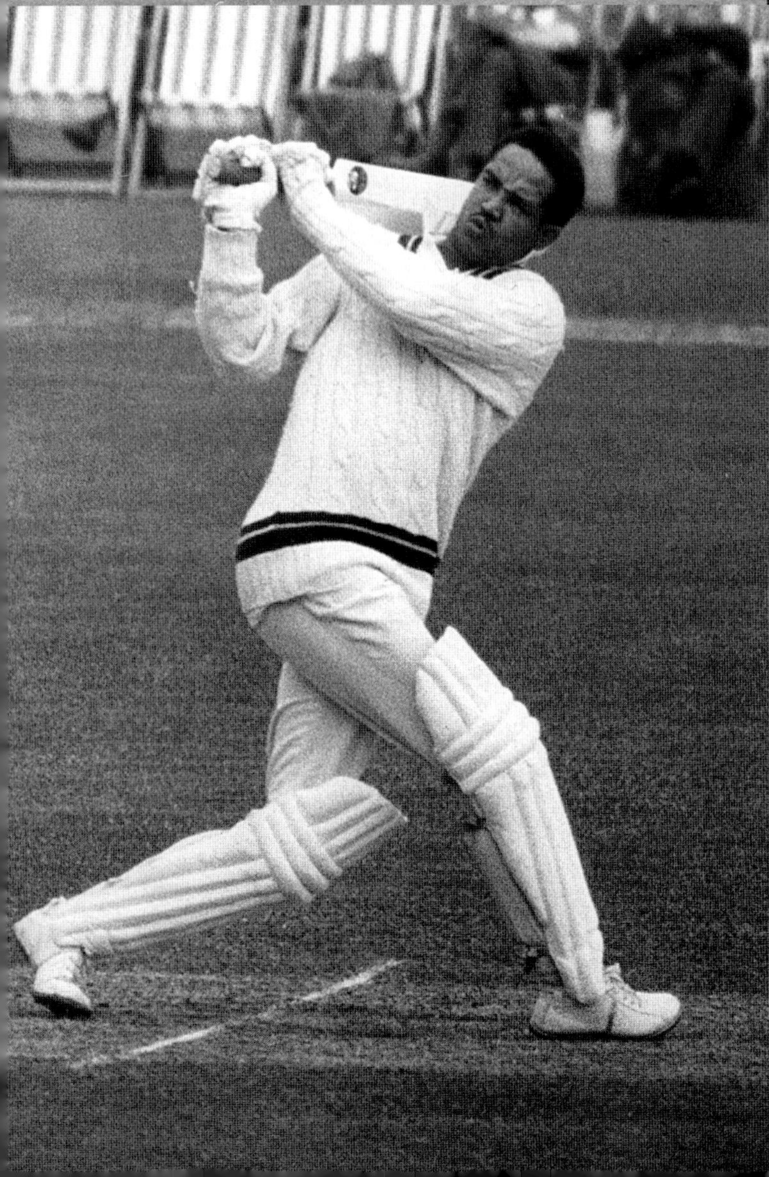
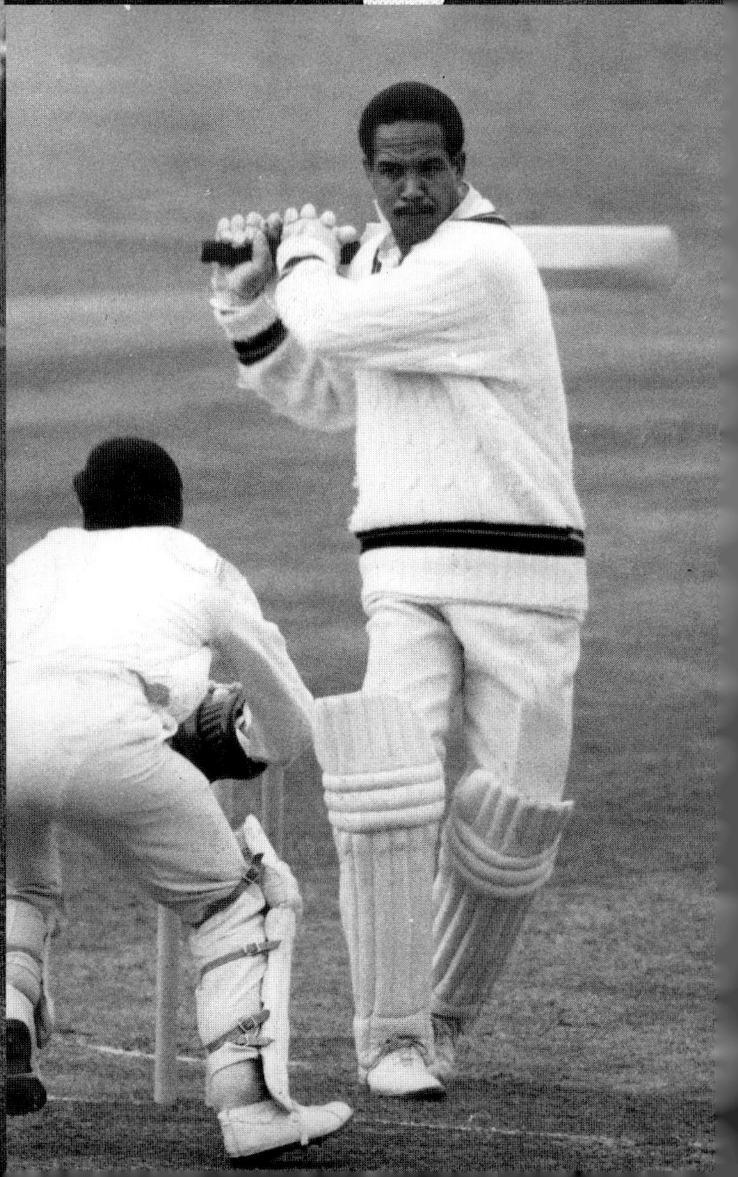

It was no mis-hit. The ball sailed over the long-on boundary – and out of the ground.

Delivery number two was dispatched a little squarer of the wicket and the third ball of this momentous over produced perhaps the best shot of all, straight back over the bowler's head into the pavilion.

At this point, according to another outstanding Notts all-rounder Bob White, the Glamorgan wicket keeper Eifion Jones said to Sobers: "Bet you can't hit the lot for six."

That was just the incentive Sobers needed… and just what bowler Nash did not want to hear.

By now he was fearing the worst. Where could he pitch the ball against a master batsman in such a mood?

He tried one down the leg side and Sobers swivelled and heaved it backward of square. Four balls, four sixes. Twenty-four runs in less than five minutes. It was awesome hitting.

Now everyone in the ground sensed that history was about to be made and an inevitable edge of tension crept in.

Nash gave Sobers a wide delivery outside off stump and Sobers' drive back past the bowler did not come out of the sweet spot. It was still a mighty blow but fielder Roger Davis was able to get under and take the catch… before stepping back over the rope.

Was it out or was it another six?

Mike Taylor, another Notts player at Swansea that day, later recalled: "The former umpire Dai Davis was in one of the stands shouting "That's out, that's out" but the rule had changed since he retired and of course, he was in."

The umpires John Langridge and Eddie Phillipson discussed the situation while the home crowd left them in no doubt that they wanted to witness a cricketing first, with chants of 'six, six, six'.

With the tension mounting Langridge raised both arms to signal a boundary.

Cheers rang around the ground, Nash looked crestfallen, Sobers had only one thought on his mind.

"Naturally, after that I was determined to hit the last one for six," he recalled. "I reasoned that he would try to change his pace and maybe bowl a quicker ball."

He was right about that. Nash, determined to get Sobers out rather than prevent him putting the last ball into orbit, gave him a straight ball which dropped short of a length.

Sobers pounced on it in a flash, opened his shoulders and pulled it square. The ball sailed out of the ground, into St Helen's Avenue and, according to the ecstatic BBC commentator, was on its way to Cardiff.

England opener Brian Bolus recalled that it wasn't until a couple of days later that a little boy who had picked up the ball in the street, brought it back to the ground. "It was a wonderful occasion, a great privilege to participate in."

Thus was recorded the first occasion of six sixes in an over. It was part of a 31-minute 76-run innings by Sobers that contributed to a 166 run Notts victory.

The man at the other end of the wicket for Notts that day was John Parkin,

Various pictures of Gary Sobers in action.

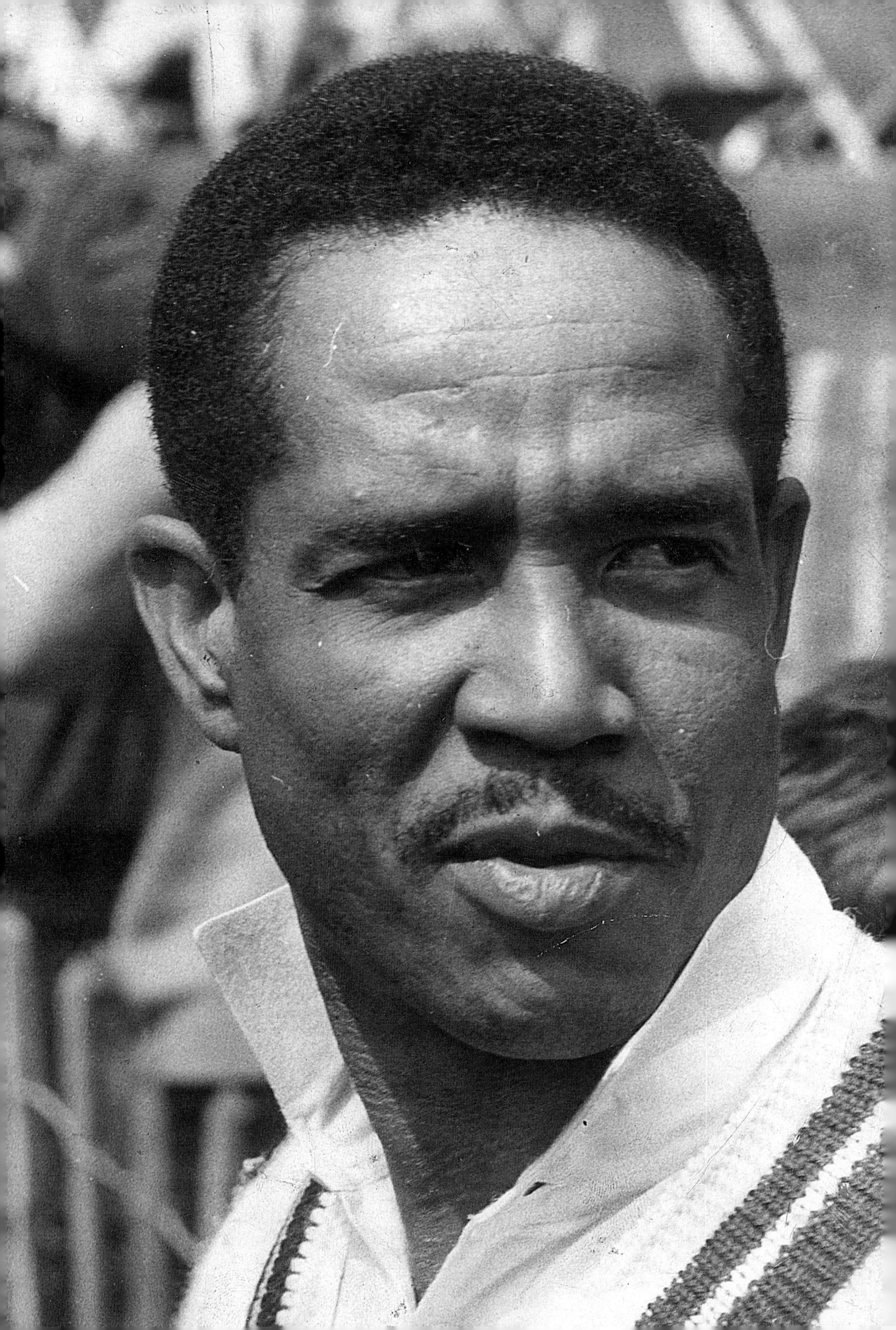

a young hopeful looking forward to a big score himself… until Sobers launched his attack.

"In the previous over I had hit Malcolm Nash for a four over extra cover and thought I was on my way.

"Then Gary came up to me, said we'd give it another ten minutes and, of course, I never got another ball."

The Palais de Danse.

Chapter Eleven
The Dancing Years

THERE was a time between the wars, when Nottingham was regarded as the dancing queen of the Midlands.

In those golden years, virtually every street in the city had its own dance band with names that many of today's dancing pensioners will remember with great fondness.

George Hames, Bradleys Syncopaters, Sissons Gaiety Band, Mrs Cave's Dance Band, Len Adkin, the Debonair dance band, Stan Richmond, Ted Bee and his Bussars, the OK Revels, The Savonias... the list is almost endless.

Nottingham had five ballrooms, accommodating 1,200 dancers.

In addition, four public baths were fitted with dance floors and every schoolroom and church hall, even works canteens, were utilised on occasions for people to dance the light fantastic.

The Hancock Formation Team in action at the Palais in 1959.

The BBC TV *Come Dancing* programme was broadcast from the Palais in 1964.

The Palais was renowned for attracting the best dancers, the Astoria for attracting the best bands including Ted Heath, Ken Mackintosh and others.

Billy Merrin and his Commanders were early regulars at the Palais, Fullerton Wills' band played at the Victoria Ballroom.

Vincent Norman was resident at Greyfriars Hall which later evolved into the Astoria, then the Sherwood Rooms, MGM, and now survives as Ocean.

Eric Harrington's band was at the Ritz ballroom – later the Odeon but now a thing of the past –and Rube Sunshine had a band at the Elite.

The Hippodrome, Empire and sometimes the Theatre Royal also featured bands while light music was part of the scene at the Mikado Café, Lyons Café, Long Row Cinema Café and, in the evenings, at Yates Wine Lodge.

The jewel in the crown was most certainly the Palais de Danse which first opened its doors in April 1925 – and actually celebrated its 75th anniversary by teaming up with Bygones and the *Evening Post* for a special tea dance.

It had been built on the site of a prison, the old Nottingham House of Correction and today is a listed building.

Dancing on that opening night was to the music of Sid Reubens and his Savanna Band,. In 1931 Billy Merrin made his debut and others to follow included Jack Hylton, Henry Hall and Harry Roy.

Among the thousands of dancers who glided across its beautiful wooden floor was the late Duke of Kent, while the Duke of Windsor was also seen at the Palais one evening.

Come Dancing 1967-style, from the Palais.

The giant globe on top of the Palais was the first and only one of its kind in the city, It used to flash red, white and blue until air traffic control at East Midlands Airport objected.

But the thing most people remember is the fountain which used to stand in the middle of the dance floor until rowdy students filled it with soap powder and the management decided it had become too much of a hazard.

In later years the Palais would be renowned for its revolving dance floor in what was known as Cupid's Bar and La Paloma before disco came along and it became the Bali Hai.

Two other features worthy of mention are the stag room where Mr Albert Mansfield would preside as men would shave, have their trousers pressed, their shoes shined, all for free... plus a little tip for Albert.

And there were the Sixpenny Partners, dancers who would take to the floor with shy, unattached clients for the payment of 6d.

One such dancer was Mae Walmsley. She became the Palais's first Sixpenny Partner in the late 1920s but got her big break when legendary dance band leader Victor Sylvester came to judge a contest and asked her to take the floor with him.

He was astonished by her natural talent and he guided her career, taking her to London where she teamed up with Sydney Stern to form a championship

Bill and Bobbie Irvine, world professional dancing champions, give a demonstration at the Peggy Payne and Audrey Bromage schools of dancing charity dance at the Sherwood Rooms in 1972.

dancing team who won five English titles and in 1930 in Paris where crowned world champions in three different categories.

She travelled the world, dancing, teaching – including members of the Royal family – and opened a West End club.

After a wonderful career in dance, she took up floristry before retiring to West Bridgford.

Any resume of dance bands in and around Nottingham would not be complete without reflecting on the remarkable career of Cyril Stapleton, the son of a plasterer's labourer who rose to the very top of the musical profession and was once described as "the world's greatest" by Frank Sinatra.

Cyril Stapleton was a child prodigy.

It was the gift of a 15 shillings fiddle from his grandfather that set the Bath Street and Morley school lad on the musical trail to the top.

At the age of 12 he promoted his own concert at the Mechanics Institute, netting a profit of £8 10s. The year was 1926.

He left school at 14 and became a cinema violinist and also a member of Nottingham's pre-war broadcasting band led by Billy Merrin.

Thanks to the generosity of Nottingham music lovers, he was able to travel to Prague to study and also won a scholarship to Trinity College of Music in London.

By the time he was 20 he was leading his own band and later took part in the first Henry Hall broadcasts.

In the 1930s he moved to London, playing at the London Casino with Jack Hylton, but it was the outbreak of war that changed Cyril's life.

He spent the war years conducting RAF bands all over the world.

He might only have achieved the lowly rank of corporal but he earned a unique place in history as a member of the RAF Symphony Orchestra invited to play for assembled statesmen at the Potsdam Conference.

Chief guests were Churchill, Stalin and Truman, the American leader actually joining the band for a Mozart minuet, with him at the piano.

Cyril returned to Nottingham after the war, as resident band leader at the Astoria where he stayed for five years before he was given the chance to take charge of the newly formed BBC Dance Band.

He worked with a galaxy of stars including Nat King Cole, Sarah Vaughan, Guy Mitchell and twice with Frank Sinatra.

He made regular visits to Nottingham with singers like Ronnie Hilton, Marion Ryan and a newcomer by the name of Des O'Connor.

If Cyril Stapleton had a fault it was that he was a workaholic and that perhaps contributed to his untimely death at the age of 60 in 1974.

Chapter Twelve
Justice

JUST imagine the lady's surprise.

She had travelled from Australia to Nottingham, trying to trace the route her ancestor had taken from the old country.

Documents had led her to Nottingham's Galleries of Justice, the remarkable museum that is a living reminder of an age when justice was swift and not always fair.

She was one of many visitors to the museum who come looking for a link with the past, to find out what their forebears endured after being sentenced to transportation from the Shire Hall courts in which the museum is now housed.

Her tour took her to the court chamber where sentenced was passed, down into the cells where prisoners were held while they waited for the transport which would take them on the first leg of a 12,000 mile journey. For the majority it would be a one way ticket.

Then she was taken into the yard, past a replica of the gallows which were put to frequent use in those unenlightened times.

Around the walls of the yard, she gazed at the graffiti, names scratched into the brickwork which have survived for more than two centuries.

And then she found it... the name of her ancestor, etched into the stone as he had waited to be taken through the transporters' gate above Cliff Road and down an iron staircase into waiting wagons.

As they were being loaded into the horse drawn trucks they were given a moment to look around, perhaps see loved ones waiting to wave them farewell, before they climbed on board the covered wagons.

The prison was located behind the Shire Hall, facing Narrow Marsh where "the ponderous walls rise in awful succession, four storeys high," according to Blackner's 1815 history of Nottingham.

Blackner chooses the story of two sisters, imprisoned for 12 years on a point of conscience, to illustrate the harsh reality of justice.

The sisters were members of a religious cult which had sprung up in the village of Calverton and which did not hold with the marriage ceremony of the established church.

When they refused to marry in the conventional way, and to legitimise their many offspring, the two women were jailed.

According to Blackner, the notoriety brought shame on an unyielding Church of England.

The women were only freed by connivance. In 1798 when the prison wall was being rebuilt, the door was left open, the women were advised to take advantage of the situation, and they fled.

Former executioner Syd Dernley with his macabre collection of memorabilia.

The model of a set of gallows Syd Dernley made as he prepared for his first execution.

Shire Hall – public executions were held on the steps.

Blackner wrote: "Thus ended the most extraordinary imprisonment which has disgraced British annals since the revolution in 1688."

In their literature the Galleries of Justice states that a gaol has existed on the site since at least 1449.

Blackner's 1815 history concludes that the prison was actually built during the reign of King John, more than 200 years earlier.

Whatever the truth, there can be no argument that thousands of people entered the building with a sense of dread for their future.

Above the door of the court house a carved smiling face looked down to greet suspects as they walked in.

JUSTICE

A frowning face graced the prisoners' exit.

The steps were used for public executions when more blood than the condemned was spilled in the crush to witness their fate.

The 1800s in particular was a time of harsh and crude justice.

Early records tell of a girl of 19 being whipped in the town for false pretences and a middle-aged woman receiving the same public sentence for keeping a brothel.

And in the worst example, Mayor Thomas Trigge was prosecuted after having a woman ducked in the ducking stool for prostitution. His sentence? He was left to the mercy of the mob.

The Luddite riots of 1811 to 1817, in which gangs of men deliberately smashed framework knitting machines as the advent of organised factories threatened the end of cottage industries, also kept the courts busy.

Ringleaders were executed and others sent for transportation.

Throughout the 1800s, the custodians of the law in Nottingham took stern measures to combat the growing problem of juvenile crime. Records show a teenager being sentenced to 21 days hard labour for stealing 4d from the New Inn.

A 16-year-old by the name of John Bush was given six strokes of the birch for stealing a tin of condensed milk.

At the other end of the criminal scale came the murderers and Nottingham had its share. John Brooks, the Lenton Murderer, pleaded for his life by telling the court he had intended to kill himself, but his victim had dissuaded him with the cry "No jack, kill me first rather than that."

Brooks said: "In a momentary fit of passion I plunged the razor into her throat, when we both fell towards the ground. I heard a gurgling in her throat

Part of the façade of the old Shire Hall.

The exercise yard – on the wall a family from Australia found grafitti written by an ancestor awaiting transportation.

and saw her hand held up to it. It seemed to me the best thing to draw the razor across her throat again."

Needless to say, Brooks was executed.

As was Joseph Tucker who set light to his wife's skirts after dousing them with inflammable liquid. He was another destined for the gallows.

In the 1950s, Mansfield pit worker Syd Dernley was one of the men responsible for carrying out the ultimate sentence.

He sent 30 men to their deaths, including the pathetic Timothy Evans who had been convicted for the murder of his wife, a murder later attributed to the evil John Christie.

In his autobiography The Hangman's Tale, Syd wrote: "I have no regrets about what I did and I sleep pretty soundly in my bed."

Syd Dernley, who worked as a welder at Sherwood Colliery, got his unusual part time job by writing to the Prison Commissioners and attending an interview at Lincoln jail.

He was remembered as a kindly man, who enjoyed a pint and a joke, and a devoted husband of more than 50 years to Joyce.

He never talked about his job. Joyce once recalled: "He would get a telephone call saying he was needed and he would go.

"When he came back a couple of days later I would ask if everything was OK. He would say yes and we spoke no more about it."

Syd Dernley was officially appointed as assistant executioner in January 1949 and bound to the King for the sum of £50.

His first duty was at Holloway Prison… to hang a woman named Margaret Laughland Williams, a young bride who had stabbed her husband after three months of a drunken and violent marriage.

Down in the dungeons.

She had pleaded self defence and Syd was uncomfortable about the prospect of hanging her. He was mightily relieved to hear she had been reprieved.

He had another false start before finally being called to Durham to assist in the hanging of two men who had murdered two local women in separate, brutal crimes.

"I was in sombre mood as I set out for Durham... I was conscious of the fact that I was set on a course which would change my life irrevocably."

Syd took a pride in his work, once recording a time of only seven seconds to carry out a hanging, but at Durham things did not go according to the executioner's manual.

As one terrified, hooded victim waited on the trapdoor, the noose around his neck, his arms and legs strapped tight, there was a delay in bringing the other man to the gallows.

The waiting man began to sway and it took nearly a minute to complete the sentence.

Syd later wrote: "The two men died cleanly but by God it had come close to a shambles."

Syd's seven second hanging came at Hull when a man named James Inglis was sentenced to death for killing a local prostitute. As the execution party escorted him from his cell, he actually began to run towards the gallows, forcing Syd and senior executioner Albert Pierrepoint to do likewise.

Syd had an unquestioning confidence in the justice and deterrent of the death sentence and even the apparent miscarriage of justice in the case of Timothy Evans did not shake his belief.

Although Evans was given a posthumous pardon, Syd later wrote: "So was Evans innocent? No one asked Pierrepoint or myself... yet if a man does not reveal the truth about himself in the moments before he goes to his death, when will he tell the truth?

"If the world of nightmares had become reality, if a man was being executed for a crime of which he was guiltless, surely he would protest, surely he would scream his innocence with his final breath."

After his career as an executioner was over, Syd and his wife ran a post office in Mansfield. He died a contented man in 1994 at the age of 73.

Chapter Thirteen
Wembley Wonders

NOTTINGHAM Forest's march on Wembley brought them FA Cup glory in 1959, for the only time in the 20th century – but it very nearly ended at the first hurdle.

They were drawn away in the third round, to London amateurs Tooting and Mitcham United.

On a freezing cold January day, Forest were given a warm Tooting welcome… and then got a sharp kick up the backside.

The Tooting programme notes proclaimed: "This is the biggest day in our 70 years of history and we are proud to entertain our illustrious First Division visitors.

"Forest have a name for clean, classic football which should be a privilege to see."

But a rock hard, rutted pitch, covered with snow, was no place for classic football. Forest were on a hiding to nothing, as the programme had pointed out that no First Division side had ever lost to an amateur club in the FA Cup.

How close Forest would come to a unique place in the record books was about to unfold.

Roared on by more than 14,000 fans, Tooting incredibly went 2-0 up by the break and the Press hounds sensed a sensation.

It took a freak own goal and a dubious penalty, scored by Billy Gray, to retrieve the situation and bring Tooting back to the City Ground.

But the amateurs had had their moment, as goals from Roy Dwight, Stewart Imlach and a towering header from Tommy Wilson emphasised, Forest winning the replay 3-0 in front of 42,000.

Next up came Grimsby Town. More than 34,000 watched a comfortable passage into round five for the Reds, Billy Gray netting twice, Geoff Whitefoot and Wilson the others in a 4-1 win.

If the win over Tooting had been a dramatic affair, the fifth round tie with Birmingham City took on the shape of a saga before Forest progressed in spectacular style.

The first game was played at St Andrews in front of more than 55,000 fans.

City scored before half-time and as the game wore on, it looked like Forest would fall to their Midlands rivals. But with just a minute left on the clock, Tommy Wilson got his head to a cross and put the ball past Gil Merrick in the home goal.

Four days later, more than 39,000 packed into the City Ground for an equally dramatic replay.

Jack Burkitt of Forest and Syd Owen of Luton exchange pennants, watched by the referee... Mr Clough!

Scoreless after 90 minutes, City scored first in extra time but Roy Dwight levelled things with five minutes to go.

Episode three took place at Filbert Street. Forest produced an inspired performance in front of 34,000, Dwight scoring a hat-trick and Billy Gray getting the other two in a 5-0 victory.

The sixth round paired Forest with the cup holders Bolton, led by the Lion of Vienna Nat Lofthouse, who had bundled his way into FA Cup history with a goal against Manchester United a year earlier which would not have a hope in hell of being allowed by a 21st century referee.

But it was a different game in those far off days. A heavy leather ball, hefty boots with wooden or leather studs... and no substitutes, as Forest would find to some cost in the final.

But they had to get past Bolton first and in front of 44,414 fans Forest did just that.

Tommy Wilson put them in command after only three minutes with a characteristic header, scored a second just before half-time and although Brian Birch pulled one back for Bolton, the Reds hung on for a place in the semi finals.

Preparation for the Hillsborough clash with Aston Villa was hardly ideal, Billy Walker resting some of his team for a game against Birmingham who exacted a measure of revenge for their cup defeat by thrashing Forest 7-1.

Roy Dwight scores for Forest.

Forest would not suffer a similar humiliation in front of their own fans until the relegation season of 1998-99 when Ole Gunnar Solksjaer scored four in Manchester United's eight goal win.

Still, back in the '50s, if you couldn't win the league, there was only the cup to bother about, so Forest gave that their full attention.

A gate of 65,000 packed into Hillsborough for the game, pitting manager Billy Walker against Aston Villa, the side he had helped to FA Cup victory nearly 40 years earlier.

Forest were the slight underdogs and were often on the back foot but Chick Thomson was in great form in the Reds' goal, saving brilliantly from Gerry Hitchens, soon to make a name as an early footballing pioneer in Italy.

In the 65th minute came the game's decisive moment, when inside left Johnny Quigley scored a spectacular goal to win the game and send Forest to their first FA Cup final for more than 60 years.

Of the six semi-finals Forest have contested at Hillsborough, the '59 victory remains their only success.

Now they had to go one better and finish the job off against Luton Town at Wembley.

On the day, the city centre was silent. Thousands made the journey south to cheer on their favourites while the rest of the Red side of Nottingham found a television set or radio to sit around.

The team chosen by Billy Walker was: Thomson, Whare, McDonald, Whitefoot, McKinlay, Burkitt, Dwight, Quigley, Wilson, Gray, Imlach.

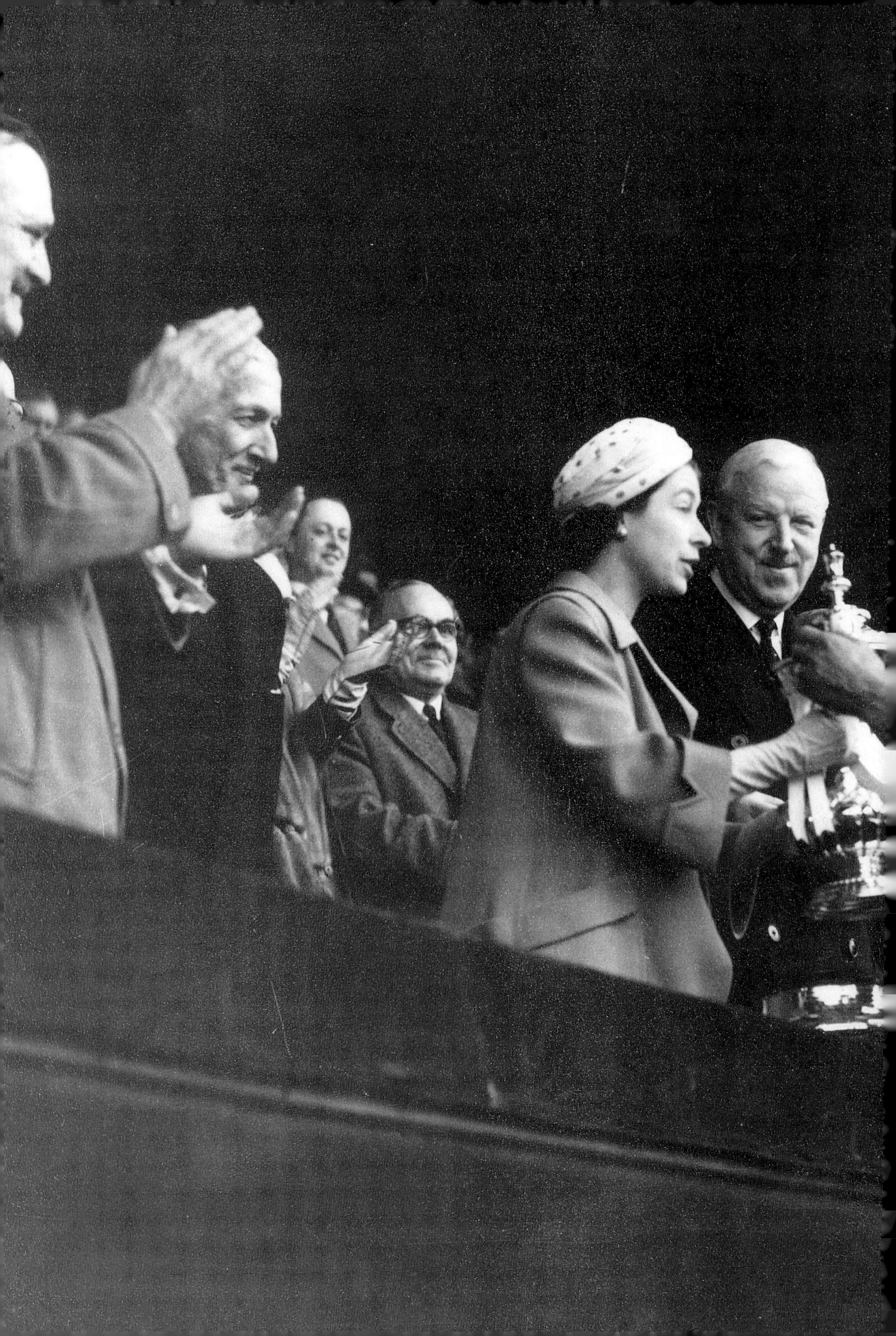

Captain Jack Burkitt receives the cup from the Queen.

The luckless Dwight is carried off, having suffered a broken leg.

They travelled up Wembley way in a red and white bus driven by Charles Stevenson of Woodborough Road, parting the hordes of fans in their red and white or black and white favours and through the giant gates.

It was a tremendous scene as the two teams came out, Forest opting to wear tracksuits over their playing kit until the last possible minute.

It was one of those glorious occasions when the Queen was the guest of honour and she was about to be served up with as exciting and tense a cup final as there has ever been.

That it was provided by two supposedly 'unfashionable' sides, merely added to the legend.

Opposing captains Jack Burkitt and Syd Owen exchanged pennants and then the referee, Jack Clough, got the game underway.

Forest produced 20 minutes of vintage, irresistible football, exploiting Wembley's wide open spaces, delighting in the perfect surface which aided the simple passing game Walker had instilled.

Nine minutes: Dwight moves in from the right wing to take a pass on the penalty spot and fire a left foot shot past England keeper Roy Baynham.

Burkitt is interviewed by a young David Coleman.

Thirteen minutes: Billy Gray sends over a left wing cross to the far post and Tommy Wilson heads down and across Baynham. Forest are two goals to the good and in dream land.

Luton were being completely outplayed and could have been on to a hiding. But in the 34th minute tragedy struck Dwight. As he broke clear Luton's Irish defender Brendan McNally got in a last desperate tackle to halt the Forest man.

Dwight went down and needed lengthy treatment before he was able to get back on his feet. But he then collapsed again, clearly in agony. His match was over, the Wembley injury jinx had struck again.

Dwight was rushed to hospital with a broken leg, but years later, said he had refused to allow the doctor to operate on the injury until after the game was over. Instead he watched it on a hospital television… surrounded by Luton fans.

The no substitute rule proved crucial. Forest had to battle on for nearly an hour with only ten men. As they tired on Wembley's stamina sapping pitch, so Luton got stronger

Irish winger Billy Bingham, later to be a manager at Mansfield Town, and centre forward Allan Brown, himself destined to take over at Forest, were a constant menace as Forest fought a backs to the wall rearguard action.

Luton broke through with a shot by Pacey which beat Thomson and the final minutes were unbearable as Luton strived for the equaliser and Forest fought manfully to keep them at bay.

Nottingham turns out to welcome the cup heroes home.

It was a memorable final and although today, more than 40 years later, it doesn't get mentioned alongside the Matthews final, Trautmann's broken neck or United's appearance post-Munich, it should rightly rank as one of the best ever seen at Wembley.

The fact that it took Forest nearly 20 years to achieve another meaningful trophy, guarantees the class of '59 a place in the club's all-time heroes book and none of the 50,000 who turned out on that Sunday to welcome the team back to Nottingham will ever doubt that they were made of the right stuff.

Jack Helyer, the city's celebrated cinema organist.

Chapter Fourteen

The Silver Screen

CINEMA is booming in Nottingham – but the face of cinema has changed beyond all recognition.

Once upon a time, the city had 52 separate picture houses from Hyson Green to Sneinton, West Bridgford to Bulwell.

Today, all but one have gone and even the survivor, the Savoy in Derby Road, has had to follow the trend. Multi-plex, multi-screen… call it what you will, that is the way of the cinema world in the 21st century.

Lots of movies are being produced and cinemas with up to a dozen screens are opening all over the country to accommodate them.

Nottingham's latest, opened in the early part of 2001 is The Cornerhouse, built on the site of the old *Evening Post* in Forman Street but a very modern addition to the city's architectural and entertainment scene.

A far cry indeed from the final days of the 19th century when the marvel of moving pictures first arrived in Nottingham.

In 1895, the brothers Louis and Auguste Lumiere had devised a single

The Adelphi cimema.

machine suitable for projecting the long strips of 35mm film produced by George Eastman.

Their first public demonstration came in Paris, followed by London, and in October of 1895, Edison's Kintoscope brought the phenomenon to the Goose Fair, in those days held in the Old Market Square.

When the first pictures were shown, it was recorded that the audience in the front row lifted their feet off the floor when a wave was about to break on the film to ensure they kept their feet dry.

The following year, the Grand Theatre in Hyson Green became the first to stage a public screening of Lumiere's films, a week's run preceding the stage production of Trilby.

In September of the same year, the Palace in Market Street began a six week run with a programme of 50 short films presented by Robert Paul. At the October Goose Fair, Randall Williams became the first showman to exhibit a Bioscope exhibition.

The new medium was struggling to gain a foothold with a public still loyal to the excitement of music hall and live entertainment. A Kintoscope parlour was established in Long Row but it was short-lived, there were occasional film shows at the Mechanics Hall and the Goose Fair continued to bring the new

The luscious interior of the Adephi, Bulwell

wonder to the public, alongside bearded ladies, two headed freaks and other incredible sights.

It was the early 1900s that really saw cinema begin to make inroads into the public conciousness.

The Palace in Market Street was renamed the Kings, doubling up with live acts and cine entertainment and Edwin S. Porter's film *The Great Train Robbery* demonstrated the power to excite through the medium of film.

In 1907 Hales Tours of the World arrived for a seven month stay in Long Row. Customers entered a replica of a railway booking office behind which stood a mock-up of a carriageway containing a screen with rear projection.

Sounds and movements of a stream train journey were all simulated to complete the illusion.

The Royal Hippodrome, which opened in 1908 as a music hall, also included cine presentations in its weekly programme but the following year the Cinematograph Act put paid to travelling shows and makeshift cinemas.

It was time to put the industry on a firmer footing and in Nottingham that meant cinemas built for the job.

The first was the Victoria Electric in Milton Street, opened on March 24 1910, followed by the Picture House in Goldsmith Street.

In 1912, the Long Row Picture House was opened, to a public fanfare with civic dignitaries turning up to admire the built-in cafes and cloakrooms… and even a full orchestra.

In 1938, this was Nottingham's newest cimema, the Cavendish, on St Anne's Well Road.

This was a boom time for the cinema in Nottingham with 27 separate picture houses going up in the years between 1909 and 1917.

A further six came in the Twenties and cinema-going in Nottingham took a mighty step forward in 1921 with the opening of the Elite, boasting 1,500 seats, a full concert orchestra, organ, two cafes, restaurant with a fountain, ballroom, smoke rooms and lounges.

On June 24 1929, the Elite became the first city cinema to embrace the new sensation. The talking picture show had been introduced two years earlier in America with Al Jolson's *The Jazz Singer*.

It was not an overnight success it has to be said. Some predicted it would never catch on and that first Nottingham show certainly seemed to prove the point. George Jessell's film *Lucky Boy* lasted only one week.

But when Al Jolson's *The Singing Fool* came along soon after, the Hippodrome spotted the potential, soon followed by the Berridge Road picture house which became the first suburban house to go talkie.

It was around this time that a new name arrived on the Nottingham cinema scene, a name that is still remembered and loved to this day.

Organist Jack Helyer in his white coat and tails entertained audiences with their favourite tunes.

For 17 years, Helyer brought music to cinema-goers at the Nottingham Ritz, later the Odeon, in the heyday of 1930s and 1940s cinema.

The Gaumont cinema, in Theatre Square.

The Vernon Picture House, Basford, pictured on the eve of closure. It had opened on January 19, 1917 and 44 years later, was to close on Saturday, September 2, 1961.

Helyer became one of the best-known organists in Britain, with some 150 broadcasts under his belt and 70 light music compositions to his name.

It was the Ritz's brand new giant Conarcher organ – one of the biggest in the country – that attracted Helyer to Nottingham in 1933.

He moved to Nuthall, where he stayed until his death in 1973.

Helyer was born in Bournemouth in 1902 to a family of eight children.

His real name was Edmund Victor Helyer. 'Jack Helyer' became his stage name when he started performing professionally, according to his only daughter Kay Williams, who now lives in Beeston.

Although Helyer didn't receive any formal musical training, it was the cardinal rule in his Methodist family that all children should learn to play the piano.

From the age of seven, Helyer's mother taught him the rudimentaries of music.

When he was 14, Helyer became an assistant projectionist at the local cinema for a wage of £1 a week.

Twelve months later he was promoted to chief projectionist.

At the same time, he launched his fledgling musical career.

Whenever the cinema's resident pianists were indisposed, he would step into their shoes.

When he moved to the Coronation Cinema in Bournemouth in 1919, he joined the orchestra as a drummer.

Later he taught himself to play the organ on the cinema's new manual organ.

By 1925, he had been appointed organist at the Electric Cinema in Bournemouth, playing for up to five hours-a-day as an accompaniment to silent films.

He moved between cinemas in Surrey, Bristol and London's Leicester Square before he heard that a large new cinema was being built in Nottingham with an impressively large organ – the four-keyboard 22-unit Conacher.

Moulin Rouge.

Unconventional, a travelling cinema.

The Ritz opened, with famous organist Reginald Foort at the keyboards. He stayed for two weeks before Helyer replaced him as resident organist.

Apart from three years in the RAF during World War Two, Helyer played at the Ritz twice a day, six days-a-week until 1950.

Helyer, who was an ardent hiker as well as a talented musician, used to open and end all his recitals with his theme tune *I'm Happy When I'm Hiking*.

In his spare time, he wrote two books about rambling and spent many happy holidays hiking in the Alps, according to Mrs Williams.

In 1950, Helyer became a victim of the decline of the nationwide cinema organ when his job was axed at the Odeon.

He was transferred to cinema management at the Gaumont cinema in Theatre Square, where he served as house manager.

Although Helyer returned to the Odeon ten years later to play a one-hour programme for the 21-week run of *South Pacific*, his performances were few and far between for the last 20 years of his life.

His 70th birthday was marked by a special 45-minute programme on Radio Nottingham in 1972.

Helyer died suddenly of a heart attack in 1973 after a trip to the Odeon cinema.

Back on the cinema scene, in 1931 the Tudor in West Bridgford opened. This

The Classic Cinema, Market Street, pictured in 1984.

took cinema to new heights with its art deco design which set the standard for future developments.

But the Tudor would survive for less than 30 years. It closed in 1959, despite a petition to save it, with the last picture show being a Carry On film while the last incidents at the cinema would involve police trying to stop people running off with souvenirs… including carpets and movie posters and pictures.

In 1933 came the opening of the city's foremost cinema, initially called the

Ritz but later known and loved as The Odeon. This was another complex to boast a ballroom and restaurant before it was forced to follow the trend and become a multi-screen complex.

It was actually the first twin screen in Europe and opened with the *Sound of Music* on one screen... and *Mary Poppins* in the other, a unique Julie Andrews double header.

It worked, the *Sound of Music* was destined to run for a record two years and two months.

Other milestones in the Ritz/Odeon history include the first production in widescreen Cinemascope with *The Robe* and the introduction of Todd-AO with the phenomenally successful *South Pacific*.

The Thirties was another boom time for the cinema, due mainly to the arrival of the talkies, with a total of 21 cinemas being built between 1931 and 1939.

The Savoy, which can now proudly claim to be the city's only surviving multi-screen independent cinema, opened in 1935.

In 1960, one of the most important events in Nottingham cinema history took place.

City author Alan Sillitoe's ground-breaking book *Saturday Night and Sunday Morning*, about life in the back streets of Radford, which had been filmed locally, was given a Midlands gala showing at the Carlton with some of the stars in attendance.

It was to set a new standard in gritty realism which would be replicated in a number of British movies during the Sixties. It also made a star out of its leading man Albert Finney.

But it was released at a time when cinema audiences were facing decline and picture houses either closed or moved over to bingo in a bid to get punters through the doors.

It has been a slow and hugely expensive job to return cinema to its golden days. It has needed a massive investment from the cinema owners. The Showcase, which opened in 1988 with a screening from the popular *Police Academy* series and the appearance of two its stars in Nottingham, led the way in new levels of comfort and customer care.

But they needed the right quality of movie to get bums on seats. The last 15 years have seen a succession of blockbusters which have succeeded thanks to the wonderful dimension of special effects.

There will be many who will remember being given cardboard glasses to watch 3-D, Sensurround sound systems, Cinerama and other gimmicks.

But the effects achieved by films like the *Star Wars* series, *Jurassic Park*, *Saving Private Ryan*, *Titanic* and *Gladiator* have taken the cinema to new heights and the future is now stronger than at any time since the golden days of the 1930s when Jolson uttered the immortal line: "You ain't seen nothing yet!"

Chapter Fifteen
Glorious Empire

A CENTURY ago, the Nottingham Empire opened its doors and the world of music hall had a glorious new venue.

The list of stars that trod the boards of the Nottingham Empire reads like a who's who of music hall legend.

Charlie Chaplin, Fred Karno, Rob Wilton, Marie Lloyd and a certain Vesta Tilly who became an adopted daughter of the city and went on to become the darling of the London and American stage.

She began life in Worcester in 1864 as plain Mathilda Tilley, born into a show business family. She came to Nottingham early in life when her father Harry became the manager of the old St George's Hall in Parliament Street. By the age of four Vesta was already treading the boards as The Great Little Tilley.

The Empire Theatre.

England footballers join in the *Lambeth Walk* during a night at the Empire Theatre just after World War Two. Lupino Lane, front left, was the star of *Me And My Girl* and also taking part were Stanley Matthews, back row, fourth from left; Tommy Lawton, dark suit, sixth from right.

It was to be the start of a glittering career in which Vesta Tilley became the foremost male impersonator of the day, feted on both sides of the Atlantic.

She made her London stage debut in 1878, earning the princely sum of £9 per night – and was forced to choose a new name when the audiences complained that they did not know if she was a girl or a boy.

A variety of names went into the hat and first out was Vesta.

From then on she became the 'London Idol' and her songs like *Burlington Bertie* and *After the Ball* were the chart-toppers of their day.

Her immaculate appearance in a wide range of roles set the fashion in every town she visited, with Vesta Tilley waistcoats, Vesta Tilley cigars and Vesta Tilley cufflinks among the most popular fashion items of the day.

Two triumphant tours of America followed with Vesta earning as much fame and success as any British music hall artiste to cross the 'pond'.

But she never forgot her roots and regularly returned to play in Nottingham, gracing the Empire stage on many occasions.

Her final appearance in the city was in 1920 at the Hippodrome when she was aged 44 and shortly after, on the final night of a month-long engagement at the London Coliseum, she announced her retirement.

After the final curtain, Dame Ellen Terry came on stage to present 'The People's Tribute to Vesta Tilley', a set of books signed by two million of her admirers.

She retired to her homes in the south of England and Monaco, became Lady de Freece, wife of MP Sir Walter de Freece and lived happily for another 44 years, until her death in Monte Carlo in 1952, at the age of 88.

One other legendary visitor to the Empire worthy of more than a passing mention is the immortal Charlie Chaplin, who was born in the east end of London in 1889.

He first appeared at the Empire ten years later as part of a clog dancing troupe called The Eight Lancashire Lads, following in the footsteps of his father who had appeared at the nearby Palace in Market Street in May 1894.

Chaplin's next visit to Nottingham came in 1904 at the Grand, Hyson Green, in a play called *Mumming Birds*. He returned to the Empire in January 1910, this time with the Fred Karno troupe.

He generally stayed at a boarding house on Bilbie Street run by Mrs Lomas, but occasionally stayed with relatives Mr and Mrs Tom Hodgkinson who lived at 100 Hucknall Road, Carrington.

Following his visit in 1910, Charlie crossed the Atlantic and eventually found his way to Hollywood where he was to become the most famous comedian in the world.

Charlie lived until the year 1975, a good 17 years longer than the Empire.

The curtain fell on the grand old theatre in June 1958. It had declined from a glorious venue for mirth and music to a run down theatre hosting strip shows and exotic dancers.

Backstage at The Empire. From the left: the King Brothers, *Heartbeat* star Bill Maynard, and on the right Issy Bonn.

The old place comes down. A demolition worker goes about his labour with a smile as he puts hard hats on these two grand old ladies of the theatre.

But though the final chapter may have been sad and seedy, the book is full of colourful chapters, legendary characters and... strange theatrical dramas.

Like the bizarre hand of coincidence that claimed the life in 1964 of bandleader William Hastings.

He died when fire swept through a theatre in the West End of London, but 30 years before, his wife May Ellen Mann had perished in strangely similar and tragic circumstances at the Empire.

She and other chorus girls were lighting a cigarette between houses when their flimsy dresses caught fire.

Although theatre staff quickly threw buckets of water over the girls, May Ellen's injuries proved fatal and two other girls were injured.

The second performance began 15 minutes late with the audience unaware of the tragedy that had unfolded back stage.

And Elizabeth Warsop, for 40 years dresser to the stars at the old Moss Empire, once recalled the night Leo the lion escaped from his cage.

"I was in my little place making tea when I was told that Leo had got loose... although I can laugh about it now, it was a terrifying experience at the time.

"I dropped my teapot and two of the stage hands carried me down the steel ladder into the stoke hold. No sooner had the door been closed than Leo stalked past. He was soon captured."

The first performance at the 1,650-seat Moss Empire was in February 1898

The Peters Sisters get close to a radiator on a cold night at The Empire.

Hundreds of the greatest stars in the history of the theatre passed through this humble stage door.

and in its 60 year history, it hosted some of the greatest performers of the era, including Stan Laurel and Oliver Hardy with their Christmas party show which also featured a young ventriloquist called Harry Worth.

In the latter years, TV stars like Frankie Howerd and Benny Hill topped the Empire bill and it also helped to usher in the rock and roll years with Tommy Steele, Terry Dene, Marty Wilde and Billy Fury.

The crowds still came, but never in the numbers as they had in the glory days of music hall before and between the wars.

Its fate was clearly sealed, TV had killed the music hall and by 1958, Vesta Tilley and Charlie Chaplin were but a memory of a rich and glorious past.

Chapter Sixteen
Service With a Smile

LIKE all big cities, Nottingham has had its share of super stores – no, not the pile it high, sell it cheap places we have become familiar with – but super stores like Jessops, Griffin and Spalding, Pearsons and Burtons.

Ironically, the name that first came to Nottingham has lasted the longest.

Jessops began as a fashion house in Long Row in 1804, opened by a London merchant by the name of John Townsend, who promised the 'gentry and inhabitants' of Nottingham 'a very choice and extensive assortment of haberdashery and millinery'.

His notice in the *Nottingham Journal* went on to say 'as he proposes manufacturing Straws, Chips and Leghorns, it perhaps may be unnecessary to say that he shall possess an opportunity of charging them on very different prices than are usually paid for those articles'.

In 1832 Townsend was joined by William Daft, son of Mary Daft who kept the Robin Hood and Little John tavern in Arnold.

But it was not until 1880 that the name of Jessop was adopted. Zebedee Jessop had joined the firm 20 years earlier and eventually became sole owner. When he was joined by his son William he put the name of Jessop and Son over the door.

Two views of the Pearsons store, one taken in 1985 and the second, after refurbishment, in 1988.

Zebedee lived until he was 83, William carrying on the business until 1919.

He earned some kind of notoriety by refusing to observe compulsory early closing, supported by his staff, and was prosecuted by Nottingham Corporation.

Although the Bench sympathised with his stance, he was fined, but still refused to submit to what he saw as an infringement of liberty.

His refusal to pay a fine resulted in a weekly increment until it stood at £10.

Still Mr Jessop refused to pay and it was reported in the Nottingham Journal, on one occasion he told the Bench: "I am a free born Briton."

The magistrates continued to fine him £10 until it stood at a hefty £128. Finally, he was persuaded by a JP for whom he had great respect, to comply with the law... and pay a nominal one guinea fine.

In 1897, Jessops moved to magnificent new premises which carried the grand name of Winchelsea House in King Street, opened hurriedly without carpets or any form of heating.

One employee Mr W.E. Gee recalled that the building had a glass roof and in the cold weather of winter, a little heating was provided by a thick gas pipe with hanging burners.

The store thrived on its new site, much due to the energy and commitment of William Jessop, until he died in 1919.

The company was run for a short time by executors of Mr Jessop's will and then became a limited company with two of Mr Jessop's sisters among its directors.

But the family ties were finally broken when it was put up for sale and it caught the eye of a young company with only two stores, both in London. In 1933 Jessops of Nottingham became the first provincial link in the John Lewis Partnership chain.

Jessops expanded its product range to include soft furnishings, carpets and

Pearsons staff outing in 1931.

hard furniture and from a turnover of just £57,000 when they took over, John Lewis built the business up until it broke through the one million pound barrier in 1956.

In the mid-'70s Jessops moved from King Street into the new Victoria Centre where it continues to hold pride of place as Nottingham's oldest super store.

It was in 1878 that Mr W. Griffin and Mr J.T. Spalding travelled up from London to buy a shop on the corner of Market Street and Long Row.

The two Londoners knew their stuff and within ten years had accumulated enough capital to start a major rebuilding scheme, helped by the acquisition of properties on either side of their shop.

A second rebuilding scheme started in 1912 and in 1924 the main Long Row and Market Street section was rebuilt in splendid style, with a facing of Portland stone.

The business remained under the control of members of the two families until 1944 when Debenhams came in with an offer they could not refuse.

It was due to two main factors that this once tiny business developed into one of the largest and best known stores in Nottingham.

First, the company always carried a large and varied stock at very keen prices – in the 1960s there was usually about half a million pounds worth of stock and the company paid 10 shillings to the first person who reported that any items were being sold more cheaply by competitors.

Second, an experienced, courteous and helpful staff offered a level of service rarely seen today. They were always at the beck and call of customers, following the policy laid down by the company which concluded: "We are the

The last days of one of Nottingham's finest stores – Burton's of Smithy Row.

hosts – our patrons are our guests. We extend to our patrons the courtesy and thoughtfulness that we do to our guests in our home."

Employees were issued with a comprehensive list of 'do's and don'ts' which ranged from never showing impatience to never applying make-up or combing hair in the store.

Employees were told: "The inflexion of voice should indicate our sincere interest and our desire to be helpful.

We do not take our handbags into departments, we do not smoke anywhere except in the staff canteen and staff rest rooms, we do not use first or last names alone, nor do we use nicknames or terms of endearment."

Pearsons began life as a 15 foot wide former ironmongery purchased in 1889 by Frederick Pearson. He bought 56 Long Row – which was known as Wigglesworth at the time – for his two sons, Charles and Tom. Stock included bright candle snuffers, curling and coal tongs, horse clippers and pig ringers, large and small.

In subsequent years numbers 54, 55 and 57 were added to create the grand Georgian fronted store still remembered with fondness by older shoppers.

The brothers were always on the lookout for innovative ideas, Tom importing rubber walled Turkish baths from America to sell at 42s 6d, while his son Laurie invented and patented the first practical and safe electrical blanket to be produced, for which he received royalties of £300 a year.

When Charles Pearson died in 1911, Tom took sole control and maintained the store's motto of 'everything for the home' but with the emphasis on quality.

His market was the well-heeled of The Park and other such suburbs and his stock reflected that. Pearsons was the first store in the country to sell Parker pens for instance.

Bustling Long Row on a Saturday morning in 1951 as shoppers mill around outside Griffin and Spalding.

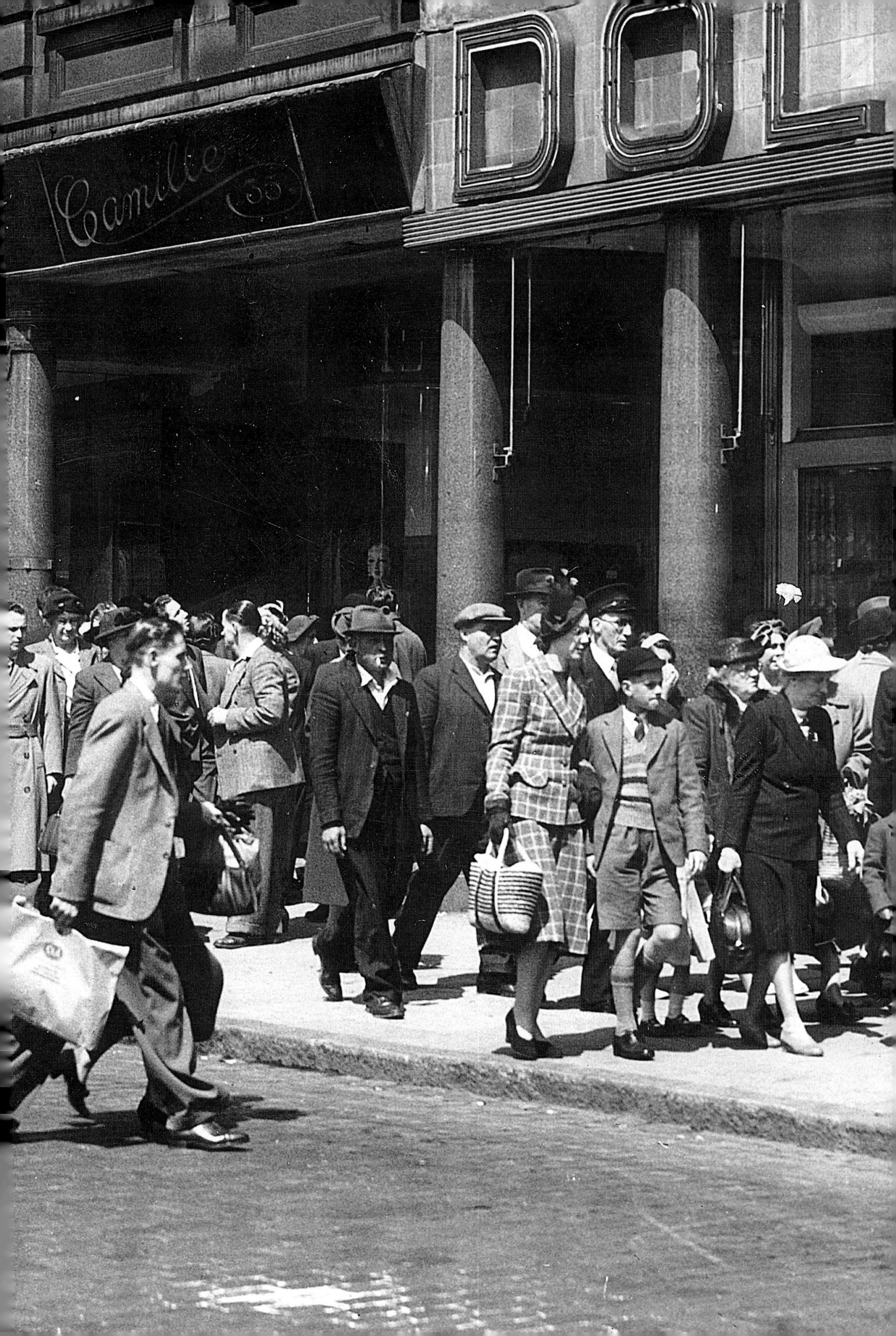
Camille
DOL

It became a pioneer in the field of electricity, actually producing its own bulbs with the company name etched on the glass.

In 1902 when King Edward VII came to the throne, Pearsons decorated the Horse and Groom public house in Wheeler Gate entirely in its own lights.

Sadly, while old Tom Pearson was a top drawer entrepreneur... he knew nothing about electricity. When time came to switch on the lights, the city centre was plunged into darkness!

Pearsons' major expansion, through into Parliament Street, came in the early 1930s when Tom had to draw on his considerable weapons of charm and trustworthiness to borrow the money from friends... with sums of £30,000-£40,000 being offered by the likes of John Player, so he could complete the project.

It is hard to imagine such an era of family-owned big business and friendly co-operation.

It was said that Major Spalding of Griffin and Spalding would always buy his pots and pans from Pearsons – and old Tom would get all his clothes from Griffin and Spalding.

It was a sad day for the city when, in 1988, the name of Pearson vanished from the city's retailing scene.

Equally lamented is the fine food emporium that was Burton's of Smithy Row.

It began modestly when Joseph Burton rode into Nottingham from his Derbyshire home, seeking a fortune. He began in a small shop on St Ann's Well Road – living in the flat above.

He had to use all the commercial knowledge he had gained in London to survive and thrive in a town singled out for its squalor and sickness, where the average life expectancy was 14-15 years of age, and where, in Narrow Marsh, stood the worst slums in Europe.

But prosper he did, opening his store in Smithy Row and cashing in on the new found wealth that the industrial revolution brought.

He established company headquarters in Talbot Street and built up a fleet of 40 horse-drawn delivery carts.

Joseph Burton opened up branches in Alfreton, Eastwood, Heanor, Coventry and Sheffield, while building up his Nottingham operation.

He took over Turkish baths in Talbot Street and converted the Victorian Halls where he opened a jam factory – only to see it burned to the ground in a disastrous fire in 1905.

But he continued to spread around the country, eventually opening 30 branches by the turn of the century.

The demolition of the old Exchange Building in 1926 led to the development of the buildings best remembered by city shoppers and for the next 50 years Burton's competed with the rest, taking in all the new innovations of self-service, frozen foods, muzak, delicatessens and so much more.

The Smithy Row store stocked 60 different international cheeses from Blue Stilton to French brie, from Swiss gruyere to Swedish chantilly; the delicatessen groaned under the weight of frogs' legs, snails, poppadums, salamis, birds' nest and kangaroo tail soup and even caviar.

Burton's also became renowned for window-dressing at Christmas and children's parties were brought to the Council House to see the wonderful displays.

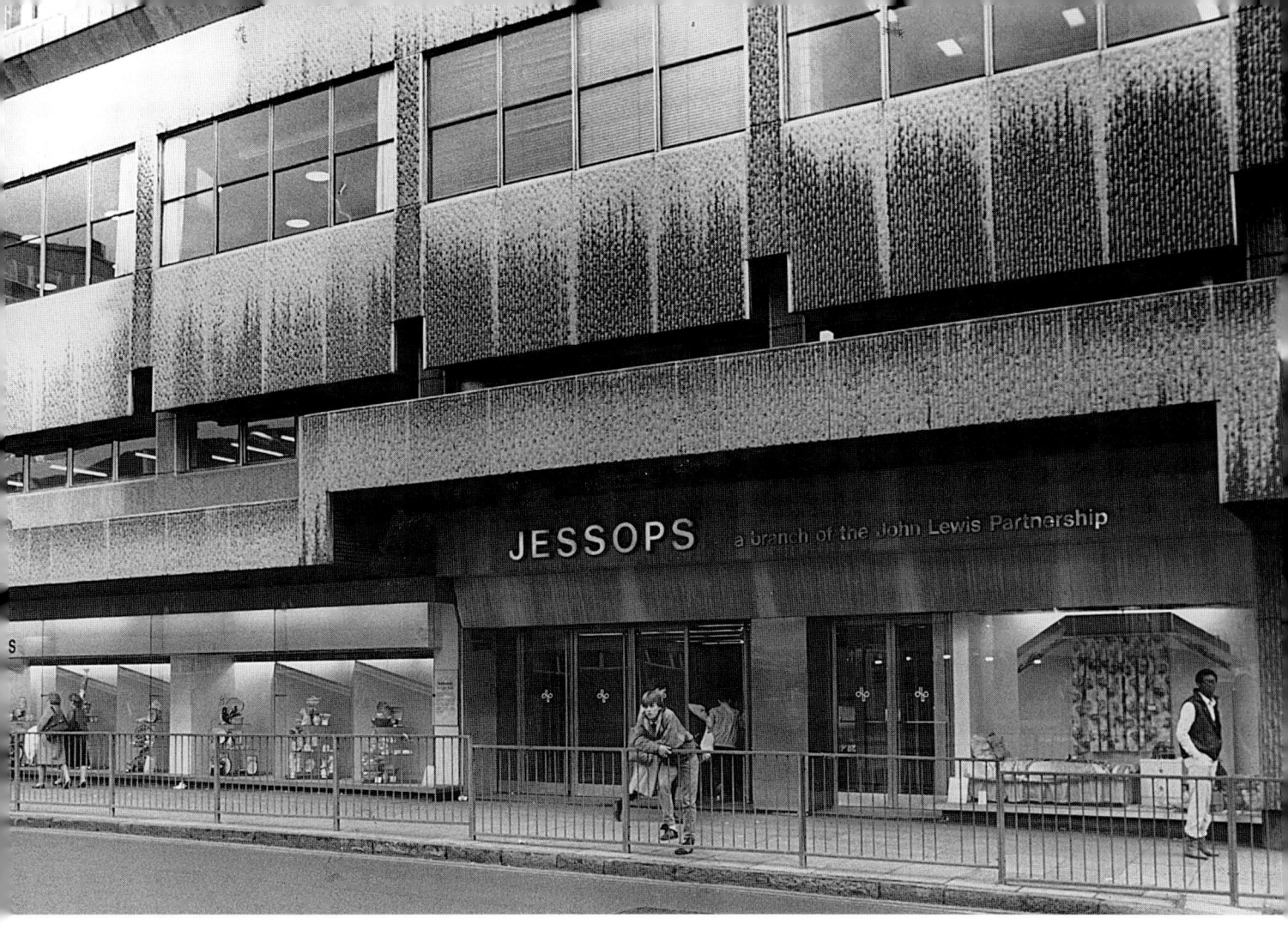

By the 1950s, the empire founded by Joseph Burton in 1858 in that St Ann's Well Road shop had grown into a 200-plus branch company.

And into the 1960s, new outlets were being established including one in Beeston which was opened by Johnny the chimpanzee,

But major changes were coming and later in the decade, Burton's of Smithy Row became part of the Fine Fare chain.

The empire of Joseph Burton had seen its best days and although it clung on to many of its customers for another 20 years, it could not hold back the tide of supermarket competition and finally, in 1983, closure was announced, bringing to an end a glorious history of 125 years service to Nottingham.

A buy-out bid by former store manager Paul Seagrave was rejected, 75 staff were made redundant and the store was closed and later split up into smaller units, an ignominious end to one of Nottingham's grandest retailing giants.

Jessops, still one of the city's leading department stores.

Chapter Seventeen
A Fine Designer

THERE are many among the people of Nottingham with memories long enough, who still weep over the destruction of the Black Boy Hotel in Long Row.

Mention the name and people shake their heads in despair that a body of elected officials of the city could sanction the eradication of a piece of Nottingham history, designed by a genius by the name of Watson Fothergill.

Fothergill left his signature all over Nottingham in the shape of his fantastic buildings, many of which are still gracing the streets of the city to this day.

But not the Black Boy. Just a stone's throw from the seat of city power, its site can be pinpointed as a memorial to the urban vandalism that typified the 1960s and of which Nottingham was as much a victim as any city in the country.

Ken Brand, a stalwart of Nottingham Civic Society and regular contributor to Bygones, described it as "one of the architectural tragedies of modern Nottingham" and there are few who would disagree with his verdict.

The Black Boy was the jewel in the city's architectural crown. Fothergill created a fantastic building of colonnades and timbered gables, a Bavarian balcony and wood balustrades – the sort of embellishments that were the great man's trademark.

The Black Boy was demolished in 1969 and it is recorded that on the day the builders moved in, tears were shed for the grand old edifice.

But although the Black Boy vanished beneath the developers' hammers, there are enough examples of Watson Fothergill's imagination left to wonder at and admire.

Certainly, we will never the see the like repeated by modern architects.

In the place of idiosyncrasies like his gargoyles and towers, decorative windows and hidden sculptures, have come the slab-sided monoliths of Maid Marian Way. It is a sobering thought that beautiful St Nicholas' rectory was demolished to make way for an office block and the historic Collins' Almshouses had to go when the road came through.

Town planners are now looking at ways to rectify the errors made in the 1960s. If and when it is done, it will prove to have been an expensive lesson and it is an amusing exercise to ponder for a moment on what Watson Fothergill would have made of it all.

The son of a lace manufacturer, he was born Fothergill Watson but reversed his name by deed poll when he was in his 50s to recognise his mother's side of the family.

Certainly, it is the name Watson Fothergill that adorns many of his most famous buildings, usually prominent around 20 feet above street level.

The great designer Watson Fothergill.

A typical Watson Fothergill creation – the Rose of England in Mansfield Road, now called the Filly and Firkin.

From the early 1870s through to 1912, Fothergill built churches, banks, pubs, warehouses and a profusion of private homes, particularly in Nottingham's exclusive Park estate.

It hardly needs a second glance to recognise Watson Fothergill's work. The bank building on Thurland Street is a classic example of his elaborate and quirky style.

Ken Brand, writing about the great man, sketches a wonderful picture of Fothergill. "The whole building has a wealth of decorative features notably, high up, three lively friezes in Portland Stone depicting farming, mining and textiles, the main occupations of the county in the 1880s."

He also added a stone monkey – a visual reference to the Victorian view of a mortgage as "the monkey on one's back."

That was just one example of Fothergill's whimsical wit.

Look for the fine figure of a medieval architect which still graces the front of his old office at 15 George Street, and the rather unflattering head of Queen Victoria at Queen's Chambers in King Street.

Over the entrance to the Parliament Street offices of the *Nottingham Daily Express*, Fothergill recognised the newspaper's Liberal leanings by incorporating the heads of three prominent politicians, including John Ewart Gladstone.

The building has been refurbished in recent years, returning it to something like its original glory. Ken Brand noticed a peculiar phenomenon, caused by using a red sand mix on the three faces which, in wet weather, can given them the appearance of over-indulgence!

Another prime example of Fothergill's work is the public house now known as the Filly and Firkin on Mansfield Road, originally built as the Rose of England, which still has a splendidly carved rose prominent above the entrance.

Fothergill the man was said to be vain, arrogant, pretentious and eccentric. One look at his buildings would provide the truth to that assessment.

He was always immaculately dressed and remembered in later life for his silk top hat, fur-collared coat and the white whiskers and beard he favoured.

But he had a great sense of humour, as his "monkey" joke surely shows.

He was a traveller, a connoisseur, a land speculator, a sportsman and, perhaps most importantly, should be remembered as a talented and significant provincial architect.

Fothergill, obsessed with his own health after the early death of his brother Forbes, reached the grand old age of 87 before he died, in 1928, and was buried in the cemetery on Mansfield Road, beneath a quirky memorial that he surely designed himself.

Opinions on Fothergill's work have ranged over the decades from amusing to naughty, vulgar to excessive.

But ranged alongside the uninspiring examples of the post-war building boom, they are an individual, striking and fascinating legacy of an extraordinary son of Nottingham.

Watson Fothergill's offices in George Street.

Chapter Eighteen
An Actor's Life

NOTTINGHAM and Notts has made a small but significant contribution to the world of entertainment – from Vesta Tilley to Paper Lace, Leslie Crowther to Richard Beckinsale, from Donald Pleasance to Peter Bowles.

But one member of the acting profession, one thespian, one giant of the stage in the grand old manner stands above all others... Nottinghamshire's only theatrical knight, the remarkable Sir Donald Wolfit.

There was no hiding Donald Wolfit's desire to be an actor.

He first trod the boards in a production at the Mount School in Newark when he was only seven, appropriately playing the part of Robin Hood.

And later, when he chance came to make a bid for the professional theatre, he cycled 19 miles from Newark to the Theatre Royal, Nottingham, through torrential rain for an interview with Fred Terry. He got the job!

Wolfit in a scene with a young Peter O'Toole.

Newark-born Sir Donald Wolfit.

A date at the Palace for his knighthood.

His story began in 1902 when he was born at 8 London Road, New Balderton – a plaque now marks the spot.

From Mount Street he won a scholarship to the Magnus Grammar School and while his studies directed him towards a career in teaching, his passion was in the theatre.

He turned his back on a teaching job in 1920 to join Charles Doran's Shakespearean Company and over the next 15 years, established a stage reputation, both in London and the provinces.

But acting wasn't enough for the great man. He wanted to be a key figure in the theatre, following the tradition of the most famous actor-managers of history – David Garrick, Herbert Beerbohnm Tree and the like. In fact, Sir Donald would become the last of that autocratic line.

His biographer – and for five years his dresser – Ronald Harwood wrote: "He was driven by a sense of service, by a belief in Shakespeare as an educative force, by a desire to take the classic drama to the community at large."

He presented his first company in 1934 in his home town of Newark and three years later took Shakespeare on tour with *Hamlet*, *Macbeth*, *The Merchant of Venice* and *The Taming of the Shrew*.

Donald Wolfit was a demanding man to work for – even his own actress daughter Margaret, felt the full force of her father's drive for perfection.

She had memories of a happy childhood but, it is recorded, that once past the stage door Sir Donald was notoriously authoritarian, sparing his young daughter even less than other junior members of his company.

But despite his strong hand, Margaret enjoyed a happy relationship with her father, even after she gave up her career as an actress upon her marriage.

And in 1993, years after Sir Donald's death, she returned to the stage, back in Newark, to perform in the Wolfit Festival Season at the Palace Theatre.

Harwood believes it was the work of Donald Wolfit and his contemporaries that kept classical repertoire alive and provided the foundation of Britain's present day theatre – in a more tangible way, he helped to restore the Robin Hood Theatre at Averham and became its patron.

He used to tour under awful physical conditions, from one end of the country to the other, to bring plays to the people.

Even Hitler could not keep Wolfit from his public.

He became a national figure during World War Two when he defied the bombs and blackouts to bring Shakespeare to the devastated population, earning headlines like Shakespeare Beats Hitler!

He was serving with the Home Guard at the time, and travelling to London three times a week ready to open his Lunch Time Shakespeare performances on October 13 1940 at The Strand theatre.

Sixty-one customers paid 1s each – the next day the theatre was hit by a bomb.

Undeterred, the company dressed on stage with Donald glorying in the discomfort and danger. The approach of enemy bombers would bring the request: "Will those who wish to leave do so as quietly as possible" …meanwhile the performance continued.

In the post-war years, his career embraced all the Shakespearean heroes and villains but it was his *King Lear* which was regarded as his finest portrayal.

Lady Wolfit signs the visitors book at the Council House watched by Sir Donald.

Wolfit had a running battle with critics down the decades, culminating in a well-publicised clash with Kenneth Tynan, but no one denigrated his Lear.

"The greatest piece of Shakespearean acting I have seen," wrote the *Sunday Times*' theatre critic.

Wolfit revelled in his position and one can picture the scene as he walked slowly towards the stage, in full costume, his dresser following with a silver salver carrying a moist chamois leather, a glass of Guinness and some peeled grapes, while lesser players stood dutifully to one side.

The advent of television and the post war frivolity of the cinema spelled the end for touring companies like Wolfit's and he did not make a comfortable transition to the movies, although he gave remarkably good performances in *Becket*, *Room at the Top* and memorably, as *Svengali*.

In 1950, Wolfit was made a Commander of the British Empire, an honour he felt was long overdue and the least he deserved after his efforts during the war, both in London and abroad.

It must have rankled that three years earlier, Laurence Olivier and Ralph Richardson had been knighted.

He would wait another seven years before the ultimate honour would come his way.

He received the news at his home near Andover, surrounded by his children and was heard to cry, in a rich Nottinghamshire accent: "If only me mum and dad could see me now."

The legend of Sir Donald Wolfit was complete. The old stage warrior's reserves of character, strength and resourcefulness had carried him from a working class home in Notts to the pinnacle of theatrical success.

For the next ten years, he continued to produce performances of extraordinary power in theatres around the world, but then, on a visit to Kenya, the first cracks in his health developed.

In January 1968, he entered the Royal Masonic Hospital in Hammersmith and he died there on February 17, at 6 am, after a series of strokes, his grief-stricken wife Rosalind at his side.

At his funeral Donald Sinden read lines from Cymbeline and at his memorial service, Olivier and John Neville gave addresses.

In his will, he left his dresser and friend Ronald Harwood £50 and the hope that he would undertake some form of biography.

Ronald Harwood summed him up thus: "No actor of his generation was surrounded by more controversy.

"He was hated and loved, dislike and admired, shunned and welcomed. He was large and yet petty, compassionate and cruel, magnanimous and mean.

"But above all, he was an actor, from the crown of his head to the soles of his feet."

Chapter Nineteen
Lawrence and Sillitoe

HOME for David Herbert Lawrence, one of the greatest figures in 20th century literature was the humble mining community of Eastwood.

It was, he once said: "The country of my heart."

He loved the green, rolling hills that stretched from Eastwood across the Derbyshire border and away as far as the eye could see – to Crich on a clear day.

His playground was the pastures and woods around his home and the villages of Annesley and Underwood, a gentle alternative to the harsh reality of mining, with its slag heaps and grimy colliery buildings, a world which never suited the thoughtful, fragile young man.

He was born the son of a miner in a cramped terraced house at 8a Victoria Street, Eastwood in 1885. His father Arthur was typical of the breed. A huge, rough man, poorly educated, prone to great rage and a liking for ale.

While he ruled the family with a barking voice and an iron fist, the young Lawrence sought the comfort of his mother's arms. Lydia Lawrence came from different stock, born into a middle class religious family who never came to terms with the life she became tied to by marriage.

Certainly, she had no desire to see her sons follow their father down the pit shaft and likely as not, she encouraged Lawrence's artistic nature to come out.

As a child, Lawrence would wander the country lanes and follow the Erewash canal. He visited the big houses of the colliery owners and recorded in his mind's eye the personalities of his youth.

He saw the deprivations suffered by the miners and recoiled at the ugly scars mining cut into his beloved valley.

Everything was recorded in his mind, stored away to be brought back to life through his pen – and almost everything he saw, sensed, experienced about his little piece of England would eventually find its way onto the printed page.

The most vivid images occur, perhaps, in his autobiographical *Sons and Lovers*, depicting his father as Mr Morel, an evil, violent man.

The family moved into their own home at 8 Garden Road, in an area of Eastwood known as The Breach which he translated into the Bottoms in *Sons and Lovers*. When Lawrence was six, the family occupied 8 Walker Street and finally 8 Lynncroft.

Lawrence's love of writing developed through his learning years at Greasley Beauvale School and later Nottingham University's original Shakespeare Street site.

Lawrence and Frieda Weekley pictured in 1926.

A famous study of D.H. Lawrence.

In 1907, he received his first payment for a piece of his writing, from the *Nottinghamshire Guardian*.

Lawrence entered a short story competition and, desperate for money, he submitted three pieces, using the names of two girlfriends to do so. One of them, *The Prelude*, won the £3 first prize.

Soon after, Lawrence left his home in Eastwood, abandoning most of his ties with the town of his birth. In 1910, his beloved mother Lydia passed away and so to did Lawrence's interest in his home.

He submerged himself in university life and into his writing, but was never far from controversy... a state of affairs that would last long after his death.

In 1912, he ran off with Frieda Weekley, the wife of his professor of language at the university (and niece of the Red Baron Manfred von Richthofen), causing a terrific scandal which Lawrence found difficult to understand.

Funded by Lawrence's prolific output, which English publishers seemed reluctant to support, the couple travelled the world. But Lawrence was dogged by ill health and on March 2 1930, at the age of 44, he died in a sanatorium in the south of France where he was buried.

But Frieda later had his body exhumed and taken back to Mexico where she had gone to live.

Lawrence's remains were eventually cremated and his ashes were interred in the town of Taos, New Mexico.

Since his death, academics and philosophers have dissected almost every word Lawrence had written, searching for answers to questions of reason and motivation.

But the simple truth is that Lawrence was an extraordinary storyteller who could transfer the images that he saw directly to the printed page so that readers saw it just as he did.

Alan Sillitoe has the same sort of genius, but while D.H. Lawrence fashioned his fiction from the fields and woods around Eastwood, Sillitoe sought inspiration in the backstreets of Radford where he grew up.

Sillitoe was raised among hard times. He remembers 'back-to-back houses... clean bricks and well appointed. A bathroom above each scullery would have completed their desirability. The streets were neatly cobbled'.

But Sillitoe also remembers the bulldozers moving in as redevelopment became the post war buzz word.

"For a time the landscape was even flatter than Hiroshima," he recalls.

Among the buildings that vanished were some of the many houses in which Sillitoe, and his family, lived for brief periods.

"They were many, because our moonlight flits were always one turn of the handcart wheels ahead of the rent man's flat feet."

Alan Sillitoe was born at 38 Manton Crescent, Lenton Abbey, and he spent his first 20 years living in and around the Radford area, St Peter's Street off Ilkeston Road and then Beaconsfield Terrace among his addresses.

He failed his 11-plus twice, left school at 14, started work at Raleigh where his parents worked, and "made holes in plywood" in a wood mill.

It was a living, but writing was a gift. While still at school, he would churn out short stories and show them to his mother Sylvie. "I always told Alan he would become famous when he grew up," she once said.

The turning point in Alan Sillitoe's life came when he joined the RAF for his National Service. He developed TB while serving in Malaysia and caught up on his education by reading hundreds of books during an enforced 18 month convalescence.

Sillitoe retired from Her Majesty's Armed Forces and with his £1 weekly pension and a wife, he headed first to the south of France and then Majorca, where the couple lived the classic under-nourished life of a starving artist.

For month after month Sillitoe pounded away at the typewriter, dreaming up

Alan Sillitoe as a young man has a pint in the Eight Bells.

novels, short stories and poems. He was full of hope but received nothing but rejection.

It was the advice of another famous author, Laurence Durrell, which finally put Alan Sillitoe on the right track.

Stick to what you know best, was Durrell's suggestion, so Sillitoe began to create a book based on his Nottingham memories.

He came up with the story of Arthur Seaton, the hard-drinking, womanising cycle worker, and a unique view of working class life that could only have succeeded because the author knew the world so intimately.

Off to the publishers went this latest Sillitoe offering – and back came more rejection slips.

But finally, some editor in London took a liking to this raw, earthy tale and, after ten years of trying, Alan Sillitoe was about to become an overnight success.

Saturday Night And Sunday Morning was an instant bestseller, its copies now numbering many millions around the world.

Two years after publication, it was filmed with equal success, Sillitoe's own screenplay helping to make a star of the almost unknown Albert Finney.

And Sillitoe did the same thing for another up and coming actor named Tom Courtenay in *The Loneliness of the Long Distance Runner*.

Since then, both stories have been adapted for stage and Sillitoe's output of novels and short stories has continued unabated.

But despite the fame and fortune and a life well away from the mean streets of Nottingham – he now lives in London – there is no doubting that his roots remain in Radford.

He returns regularly to see family and friends, have a drink, check out the latest changes to the backcloth about which he wrote so passionately.

And after 40 years or so, he revisited the world of Arthur Seaton, to satisfy a demanding public who wanted to know what had happened to the bad boy of Radford.

All is revealed in *Birthday*, yet another triumph from Nottingham's most celebrated living author.

A recent portrait of the author Alan Sillitoe.

Chapter Twenty
The General

NOTTINGHAM General Hospital, which closed in 1982, was one of the oldest in the country. Opened in 1782 after banker John Key left a legacy of £500, it came to be regarded as the People's Hospital.

Yet when it began it was run rather like a country estate with open fields to the west and north.

It had its own stables and herb gardens and in summer the pig sties wafted fruity smells below the windows of one ward.

It cared for thousands of wounded soldiers during two world wars and was a well-endowed voluntary hospital before it was absorbed into the NHS in 1948.

Records for the 1930s show it was spending £3,000 a year on coal and about £10,000 a year on drugs, dressings, instruments, including 214 miles of bandages, 72 miles of gauze, three tons of cotton wool and 100 gallons of cod liver oil.

Potato Week contributed 57 tons of potatoes and other vegetables and Egg Week produced 166,000 eggs.

Former nurse Elizabeth Swales recalled the great difficulties created by food rationing during World War Two.

"Meat, butter, cheese, bacon and sugar were very scarce and meatless days were introduced twice a week.

"A special vegetable pie with gravy was served.

"We called it Lord Woolton pie as Lord Woolton was the Minister of Food."

She added: "Carrots were very plentiful in our diet. It was said they contained a vitamin which helped us to see in the dark.

"Puddings were often baked without sugar and dried fruit and grated carrot was used to help sweeten them.

"Fish was unrationed but it was so scarce that one had to queue when a ship came in. Food queues were a way of life.

"We were fortunate at the General Hospital as several benefactors sent baskets of eggs in what were known as egg weeks.

"Many were preserved for later use. English soft fruit, apples and pears were also kindly donated by benefactors and friends of the hospital.

"The work was hard and the hours long and many were hungry.

"A proportion of our clothing coupons were surrendered for uniform. Soap and soap powder were also rationed and we were allowed two soap coupons from our ration for bathing and washing personal clothing.

"Uniform, sheets and towels were sent to the hospital laundry. Sweets were rationed and chocolate was very scarce."

The old Nottingham General Hospital.

The hospital had an auxiliary fire post inside the hospital grounds, which was manned 24 hours a day.

Large surface water pipes were also installed along the edge of the pavement with valves for the fire services.

Mrs Swales recalled: "These pipes were quite a hazard in the black-out and in icy conditions.

"Many broken legs and wrists were caused by people tripping over them and one of our nurses fell and broke two front teeth.

"Nearby there were very large tanks of water for use in air raids."

During the war the hospital entrance gates and railings were removed to be recycled into guns. Private houses also had railings requisitioned for the war.

Mrs Swales recalled the good liaison between the officers and men of the Sherwood Foresters stationed at Nottingham Castle.

"There were social activities and an exchange of invitations to functions. But there was one disadvantage.

"Night nurses' rooms were on the top floor of the nurses' homes and the band used to practice for hours in the Castle grounds, especially before special parades. Sleep was difficult or badly disturbed.

"The war years were hard, but there were happy times too and the work was interesting and fulfilling.

"There was a good family atmosphere at the General Hospital and lasting friendships made. Some continue still."

Another well-remembered member of staff from that time was Margaret

Former ward sisters of the General Hospital pictured at a reunion in 1991 with Miss Margaret Plucknett, centre, who was a former matron and had worked there from 1940 to 1958.

Plucknett who joined Nottingham General Hospital in 1940 and succeeded Miss Iris Liddle as matron in May 1941. Her first week in the post brought Nottingham's worst air raid. She recalled: "As I came up the covered way with Miss Graves, my deputy, I saw the first Molotov basket of bombs descending on our town and I wondered what the night had in store for me.

"The bombs missed the hospital – very narrowly – but brought us in some very severe burns cases from a wholesale bakery which had a direct hit.

"Everything was ready and we had a very good team. A ward now filled with casualties with terrible burns injuries and I remember in those days burns were not so easily treated.

"Extra beds were placed in all wards where possible to increase the total number available.

"The movement of patients from the top floors in case of raids had to be planned.

"The use of Cedars Hospital, Ruddington Hall and Selston Hospital (a new school taken over for the duration of the war) enabled us to keep the main hospital reasonably clear for emergencies.

"All sisters and nurses were put on a rota each night in case an emergency occurred.

"Special surgical units were planned – with a team of doctors and nurses on standby to deal with outside emergencies. A first aid post was set up in the out-patients' hall, manned by independent staff, such as Red Cross and St John nurses, plus married trained nurses, to deal with minor injuries.

"They were a tremendous help. Further extensive plans had to be made for a shadow hospital in case the General suffered a direct hit.

"Increased bed numbers, plus the quick turnover of patients, meant extra linen – an emergency stock was kept which the ward sisters could call on at any time.

"We also had an emergency stock of drugs and dressings.

"The Linen Guild and its members gave marvellous support and a first class sewing party was held at the home of Mrs Kaplowitch in The Park.

"Convoys were not as numerous as we had anticipated but D-Day casualties came our way from units pressing towards Caen and at another time we had a convoy of German prisoners.

"Another convoy brought in the son of Mr and Mrs Frank Wills of Bristol – known to me because of the wonderful Wills involvement with the Bristol Hospital I had served for several years.

"We in Nottingham had the generosity of the Player family – Mr W.G. Player was chairman of the committee at the General and Mr John Player was another great benefactor for the Pay Bed Wing and the Children's Hospital.

"And on to the birth of the National Health Service in 1948. We welcomed the NHS with reluctance, much as a large private firm doesn't 'relish' takeover bids today.

"Nevertheless we realised it was 'progress', meant for the benefit of hospitals and for the eventual benefit of the general public.

"We were a well endowed hospital financially with friends galore. We realised, however good the intention of the NHS, that life for us could never be quite the same again.

The General Hospital's former outpatients department in The Ropewalk.

"We no longer had total independence. New administrative rulings and new administrative departments emerged.

"Mr H. M. Stanley, the hospital secretary and house governor, was a nice man who cared about people.

"We got on very well, and I had great respect for his assistant Mr Cyril Reddaway.

"The Regional Board assumed responsibilities for a wide range of issues, even to the choice of purchasing and linen.

"Nursing officers visited the hospitals in their region from time to time to discuss staffing limits or problems. Our hospital became one among many.

"The Nottingham General Hospital was a splendid organisation and we had a pride in its constant development to keep up with the times.

"The builders were constantly on the premises the whole of the time I was there, extending or improving a very old foundation.

"The last major development before I retired was the opening of a new Radiotherapy Department in the Ropewalk Wing.

"There have been many advances since then, of course. In my day there was no central sterilising department.

"There were no disposable syringes, dressings, operating gowns and sheets as there are today. It was a very different story. We knew the hard way but it was great."

Demolition men get to work in 1994, reducing the ugly Trent wing to rubble.

Miss Plucknett, who retired in 1958, added: "I am very fond of my dear old hospital. I had a very happy 20 years there.

"Before the NHS was introduced, Nottingham General was a wealthy voluntary hospital with wonderful friends."

In 1948 Nottingham's voluntary and local authority hospitals were taken under the wing of the NHS.

Hospitals no longer had to rely on legacies, gifts and grants but were funded through a fixed levy in the form of National Insurance.

The average cost of an in-patient for one day at the General Hospital in 1948 was £1 6s 2d. Forty years later it was £72.

Now that same NHS is well into its second half century. Since then the General Hospital has closed and many of its services have transferred to the twin centres of excellence – Queen's Medical Centre and the City Hospital.

The NHS is undoubtedly one of our most precious national institutions and the first 50 years saw remarkable advances in medical knowledge and treatment.

People are living longer. Average life expectancy has gone up from 66 to 74 while women can expect to reach 80 compared with 71 in 1948.

Killers such as diphtheria, polio and tuberculosis – four people a week were dying of TB in Nottingham in 1948 – have largely been conquered.

Sadly some things have got worse and deaths from diseases of the heart and some forms of cancers continue to pose major health challenges.

But many medical conditions which would have gone untreated 50 years ago can now be successfully tackled.

For example many patients have had their lives transformed by kidney transplants and hip replacements.

The volume of work undertaken in hospitals, health centres and the community has escalated.

Nye Bevan, one of the architects of the NHS, envisaged that demand for services would diminish as the health of the nation improved.

In fact, spending has leapt from £433m to £42 billion now – the equivalent of more than £1,000 a second for every household in the country.

During that period Nottingham's health budget has increased from less than £3m to £380m.

The NHS will never have enough money to do all it would like.

But the health service is much more than figures on a balance sheet.

It's first and foremost about people.

Chapter Twenty-One
A Man Named Larwood

HANDS hewn from a pitface in the Notts coalfield and a tiny frame that hurled cricket balls with all the venom and pace of a speeding missile. Harold Larwood was most certainly the stuff of which sporting heroes were made.

Telegrams, it would appear, played a prominent part in Harold Larwood's career.

The hot, crossed wires that sent cables of unchivalrous intent flashing from Australia to England were certainly the stuff of which Empires were unmade back in 1933.

And all because, by all accounts, Harold was bowling a tad too short and fast for our Antipodean cousins Down Under.

Certainly the heated messages between the Australian Board of Control and Marylebone Cricket Club, threatening anything from a crime of passion to, even worse, a gunboat off the coast of Sydney, will command at least a chapter in the annals of the game.

Yet one of his fondest sporting memories perhaps says more about Harold Larwood than any of his stunning statistics or those historic missives across the Commonwealth that they inspired.

A quaint county match for his native Nottinghamshire against Hampshire was the setting as a far more sedate and joyous telegram arrived on the field of play. The news was good for Larwood, bad for Hants. It told the feared pace bowler that another perfect delivery – this time it was his devoted wife Lois who had given birth to their eldest daughter.

Larwood then preceded to take five quick wickets, prompting England batsman Phil Mead to say: "Harold, I'm only glad you didn't have twins!"

It's fitting that seven decades later, for his 90th and last birthday on this planet in November 1994, his wife, children, grandchildren and great-grandchildren (34 branches of the Larwood clan all told) were present to celebrate with the family figure they doted on throughout their lives.

A pipe and slippers man who drank Ovaltine before bed during his retirement years in a quiet Sydney suburb, few Aussies who knocked on his door would equate this unassuming, placid Pom with the man who terrorised Australia's best batsman and whose belligerence with a cricket ball almost had two major governments on a crisis footing.

That moment of destiny arrived during the 1932-33 Test series in Australia as England went in search of the famed Ashes, then in the possession of the home side after their victories on English soil two years previously.

Harold Larwood.

A MAN NAMED LAWOOD

In an age when the game, like society, had strict codes of class and snobbery, Larwood was the working class lad who had graduated from the north Notts coalfields to become a professional cricketer at Trent Bridge.

For the privilege of being a Player, he was paid 12s 6d per week.

The captain on that controversial Aussie tour was Douglas Jardine, Gentleman, and a man of independent means who didn't need to be paid for playing the game.

In England in those days, Gentlemen and Players entered and left the field of play by separate gates.

Jardine masterminded the 'Bodyline' or 'leg theory' tactic that almost saw the tour cancelled mid-match during the Third and bloodiest Test at Adelaide.

He chose Larwood, the fastest and most hostile pace bowler of his generation, to spearhead his plan, a strategy borne out of the fear of master batsman Don Bradman whose supremacy had done much to secure the Ashes two years before.

Larwood's front line colleague at Notts, Bill Voce, was also recruited to bowl specifically at the body, with fielders packed short and tight around the leg side of the wicket.

The Larwood family leave England for a new life in Australia.

Larwood runs in during the infamous Bodyline series.

The results were almost as startling as the Australian and Bradman's capitulation.

England triumphed 4-1 in the series with Larwood grabbing 33 wickets at 19 runs apiece, a remarkable performance by any standards but more so with Australia boasting one of the strongest batting line-ups in the history of the game.

It was at Adelaide, though, that the wires heated up and 'questioned were asked in the House' when home skipper Bill Woodfull and Bertie Oldfield were badly hurt by vicious deliveries.

Diplomacy prevailed, however, and the series continued.

The intimidatory tactics eventually won the day and the Ashes – but few friends, either abroad or at home.

Jardine, aloof, cold and upper class, refused to apologise for the way in which the Ashes were won. Larwood, the perfect pro who obeyed his captain's orders to the letter, would not criticise his skipper or tactics.

Although his place amongst cricketing legends was confirmed Larwood's international career was effectively over. And yet, it almost didn't begin.

Born in Nuncargate in 1904 and educated at Kirkby Woodhouse, a raw 17-year-old he was invited to Trent Bridge for trials by Joe Hardstaff.

Just 5ft 7in and 11 stone wet through, Harold already had a reputation as a lean and mean pace bowler for his local village side.

After 15 minutes without success in the nets at Trent Bridge, though, his single-minded, stubborn streak took over and he headed for the local bus stop and a ticket home.

Just then, so the story goes, a messenger arrived to say his father was on the way and he was taken into the committee room where a place on the staff was offered – at 12s 6d per week, it was the same amount he was paid at Annesley pit (his second job after school, after a day's potato picking on a Notts farm).

"I got the biggest dressing down from my dad I can remember," Harold once recalled. "He told me I should have negotiated something better."

Larwood became an instant hit. Between 1927-36 he topped the national bowling averages five times (a record unmatched today), this with the 'hindrance' of the most docile cricket strip in England as his home pitch.

Huge crowds flocked to Trent Bridge. The county team reporting for a spot of pre-season training would attract at least 2,000 fans.

Harold Larwood on a nostalgic return to Trent Bridge.

In 1932 he took a phenomenal 162 wickets in the County Championship at 12.86. Already a Boys' Own hero, taking 100 wickets in a season eight times, he chalked up more victims during his 21-match Test career.

During his exploits in Australia, contemporary newspaper reports revealed the Press corps 'exhausted their vocabularies in endeavouring to describe him' – both home and foreign journalists.

Famous Australian googly bowler Arthur Mailey wrote of Larwood "I cannot remember a more dominating factor in any series of Tests than Larwood's bowling. His influence on the Australian batsmen seemed to make them do strange things. This unassuming and quiet fellow was a veritable nightmare to Woodfull and company."

An injury sustained on that gruelling tour ended his Test hopes and he was forced to operate off a reduced run-up until his retirement in 1938, aged 34.

The Larwood family then headed north-west to Blackpool where Harold ran a sweet shop on the Lancashire coast. Then in 1948, fate saw former 'Bodyline' Test foe Jack Fingleton step back into Harold's life. While covering Don Bradman's final tour of England as a commentator, he drove to see his 'old adversary' after the Old Trafford Test.

By 1950 Larwood was off to Australian again – this time on a friendly mission to settle in the country.

"Jack said something about the old days in Australia," said Harold in an interview later in his life.

"I said 'By God it wouldn't take me long to get back out there'. That started it. When Fingleton returned to Canberra he saw to the arrangements.

"Right nice of him considering it were me who got him for his second duck in Adelaide.

"The scope, the space, the climate and our daughters made me want to go. There was nothing I could do for their careers in England.

"I said to them: 'In future years you'll either bless your mother and father or you'll curse them'. Turned out they blessed us, thank the Lord.

"I don't know what I expected when we landed but I was welcomed like a king. It took me back to Sydney, my last Test, when I was sent in as nightwatchman and scored 98.

"I thought the crowd would be against me after what'd happened on the tour.

But Australia had brought in a fast bowler, Alexander, to give me some of my own medicine, and I clobbered him. He got one for 140 and I bet I got half of them.

"When I got out the crowd rose, gave me a standing ovation. Me? I thought as I walked out. Then it came to me. The Aussies love a fighter."

The player whose menacing influence on the Australian team in 1933 was said to 'gleam like malignant lightning' made his home amongst those who, far from reviling him, respected and revered his immense talent and contribution to cricket's hall of fame.

Back in his native land, cricket's ruling bodies never did forgive, though Larwood seldom talked about the 'Bodyline' tour in public, even on his visits to his homeland and county.

By the 1960s, the social divisions had faded. All players came and went to the middle by the same gate. But it wasn't until a British Prime Minister and cricket fan John Major, someone with a sense of fair play, recognised Larwood's achievements and services to the game and his country.

Although nearly 60 years late, Harold Larwood's MBE award in 1993 always took pride of place in his Sydney home during his remaining years.

A belated but quite appropriate tribute to a true gentleman and truly legendary player.

Chapter Twenty-Two
The First Lord Trent

ACROSS the city flags at half-mast, hanging limp and motionless in the still morning air.

Nottingham had lost one of her finest sons... a man who had helped shape the city and make a contribution which will, likely as not, survive for centuries.

Jesse Boot, First Lord Trent of Nottingham, died at 5.45 on the morning of June 13 1931 at his home on the beautiful island of Jersey.

He was 81.

According to his friend and fellow Freeman of the City, Alderman E. Huntsman, the vision of those flagpoles capture perfectly the sense of sadness and loss.

"No artist could have wished for a more striking symbol," he told the *Post* afterwards.

The splendid frontage of a turn-of-the-century store.

Boots offices in Station Street.

"It seemed that these lifeless things shared the sorrow that lay at the heart of the city that had lost one of the greatest and dearest of her sons.

"It is safe to say that she will never know a better."

They buried Jesse Boot in a specially-made tomb at St Brelade's on Jersey, and they paid tribute to his life and achievements at a memorial service in St Mary's Church back in Nottingham.

To trace the story of Jesse Boot, it is necessary to go back to the year 1850 when he was born in Hockley, a real Nottingham east ender.

His father was a labourer whose health was wrecked for the princely sum of 12 shillings a week.

When he became too ill to toil on local farms, he opened a herbalist's shop in Goose Gate – perhaps founded on remedies he had devised and discovered in the fields in which he worked.

But he died in 1860, when young Jesse was barely ten years old. If times had been hard before, they certainly did not become any easier with his father's passing.

It is hard to believe that the man who was to build a worldwide commercial empire was forced to leave school at the tender age of ten to help his mother in the shop.

But Jesse was a quick learner and a natural businessman. By the time he was 13, he had taken over the running of the shop, lock, stock and barrel.

His formal education may have ceased at the age of ten, but Jesse Boot, raised amidst the poverty, deprivation and sickness that was Victorian Nottingham, was streetwise enough to know that to be a success, he had to sell more cheaply than his competitors.

An early example of Boots' fleet of delivery lorries.

Jesse Boot.

Tablet production at the Island Street factory.

The seeds of his business style were sown out of his upbringing.

He knew people needed drugs but could not afford to pay the ridiculously high prices that were the standard.

"My idea was simply to buy tons where others bought hundredweights or less, thus buying much more chapely, and to make all the articles I sold look as attractive as possible."

Jesse Boot dismissed criticism from his rivals by saying: "I was doing the public a much needed and appreciated service and at the same time, I was doing quite well for myself."

And he countered any possible backlash by astutely naming his business the Boots Pure Drug Company.

Jesse Boot threw his energies into the business, sometimes working 16 hours a day. By the time he was ready to float the company, in 1883, he had 11 shops and three years later he had expanded to 60 in 28 different towns.

He was, by now, 36 years old and had been working at his trade since he was ten. The labours inevitably took their toll and in 1886, he was struck down by illness.

He chose the island of Jersey to help his fight back to fitness – it proved to be the best decision of his life.

During his weeks of convalescence, he met Miss Florence Rowe, the love of his life.

They became husband and wife and returned to live over the shop in Goose Gate, where she proved to be the inspiration which carried Jesse Boot to the pinnacle of the business world.

His genius for trade was so great that by 1917 he had opened 600 retail establishments around the country and in June 1920, he celebrated his 70th birthday with the congratulations of his 14,500 employees.

Jesse Boot was dedicated to the well-being of his staff, even though he was constantly in pain from crippling rheumatism, and he used a car specially constructed for him, to tour his retail establishments.

During World War One, when Boots was responsible for the research and development of box respirators to combat German poison gasses, Jesse Boot raised money for the fighting men from his company by launching a magazine which kept everyone in touch with events unfolding across Europe.

For a year, the magazine sold in its hundreds, at twopence a copy, until the scarcities of paper and labour forced its closure.

But not before it had raised £1,350 for a sick and wounded fund.

Such was Jesse Boot's incredible appetite for work and his unending imagination for opportunities, both commercial and philanthropic.

He did not retire until he was into his seventies and despite the agonies of his illness, he was still conducting major transactions from his invalid chair or sick bed.

As he built his empire, Jesse Boot left his mark in towns and cities across the country where branches of Boots were opened.

He worked closely with architects in places like Shrewsbury, Gloucester and Windsor to ensure his shops were in total harmony with the historical associations.

But it was on his home city that Jesse Boot lavished incredible levels of support.

He gave £50,000 to the General Hospital and presented the city with its magnificent war memorial.

He gave £200,000 for a new boulevard from Dunkirk to Beeston, £10,000 for a chair of sociology at the Nottingham Congregational Institute and £50,000 towards the purchase of Woodthorpe Park.

And he gave thousands of pounds towards the building of the Albert Hall.

But the jewel in Jesse Boot's crown and which has helped spread the name of Nottingham to the four corners of the earth is the University of Nottingham.

Not only did he donate the site for the college but also £100,000 towards the buildings and £50,000 for the endowment fund.

It is estimated that his expenditure at Highfields amounted to well over a million pounds spent on football pitches, cricket squares, the lake, tennis courts, bowling greens, the largest outdoor swimming pool in England, ornamental gardens and so many other features of the campus and its surroundings.

Jesse Boot's achievements, and his generosity, did not go unnoticed or unrewarded.

He was knighted in 1909, became a Freeman of the City in 1920 and elevated to the Peerage in 1929.

This then was the life that mourners gathered to praise on that June day in 1931.

Those attending the memorial service likened it to events following the death of King Edward in 1910.

As the congregation waited in St Mary's Church, the sound of a siren cut

Boots firewatch squad pictured in 1942.

through the city air... factories, laboratories, warehouses and offices of the great man's company fell silent.

His contribution to the life and soul of Nottingham can never be underestimated, but the many tributes which were written during those sad days spoke as much about the man as the empire builder and philanthropist.

One reporter wrote: "...he has left behind a shining example of how the infirmities of the flesh may be dominated by the greatness of the spirit."

*The title of Lord Trent passed to Jesse's son John. Sadly, the line died with him in 1956.

Chapter Twenty-Three
Old Market Square

LOVE it or hate it, Slab Square is the heart of Nottingham.

Daily it echoes to the footsteps of thousands of locals and visitors alike who come to admire its size and take advantage of a traffic-free oasis in the middle of the bustling city.

For most, its history starts with the Council House which stands, dominant, facing the sun.

Designed by Cecil Howitt, it was opened by the Prince of Wales in 1929… but that is modern history. Back in the mists of time, Nottingham's Old Market Square can trace its origins to the time of Henry II.

When he granted a Royal Charter allowing a market in the town, it contained the entreaty that "the men of Nottinghamshire and Derbyshire were to come to the borough of Nottingham every Friday and Saturday with their teams and pack horses".

Henry VIII was so impressed he called it "the fairest without exception in all England", although that was not an opinion shared by all.

In 1670 the famous chronicler John Evelyn wrote of "an ample market place with an open sough, a pond in its centre and a mouldering wall down its midst, with trees, sawpits, stocks, pillory and ducking stools".

At one time, the market place had three crosses within its perimeter. The Hen Cross at the High Street end of The Poultry survived until 1801 when it became a hazard to traffic. It was demolished and its stones used in the repair of Trent Bridge. The Butter Cross stood in front of the Exchange but, according to records, did not survive beyond 1720.

The Malt Cross, between Sheep Lane and St James's Street, was an important point on the market place map, where maltsters and potters traded.

It was demolished in 1714… and sparked off a trading war that would last until the end of the century.

In the wake of the Malt Cross removal, the city fathers decided to pave the market place with boulders – and charge farmers a corn toll to pay for the dubious improvement.

Predictably, the farmers weren't fussed with the idea so they came up with a crafty dodge, bringing only a sample into town for prospective buyers to view.

Back came the council with a chain of toll houses and collectors on the outskirts of town. They would follow delivery carts to the premises of the buyers and then charge tax before the sale was allowed to go through.

With passions simmering, the council rebuilt the Malt Cross by way of appeasement but it would be 1799 before the row was settled and the market place was once again declared toll free.

The imposing grand staircase from the ground floor of the Council House.

But it did not last long. When the council paved the square in 1826 to ease the chaos of the weekly market, they raised stall rents to pay for the improvements and as prices crept up the traders retaliated by taking their case to the highest court in the land, but the Court of the King's Bench sided with the local authority.

During the 1800s, the market stood every Wednesday and Saturday, bringing prosperity to the city centre.

It absorbed the intrusion of horse drawn trams without too much trouble, but it was the advent of the electric tramcar which would mark the beginning of the end.

Fish, fruit and vegetable stalls were re-sited in Sneinton as an army of labourers changed the face of the square with new tracks, overhead poles, signs and islands, hemming the traders into the centre.

The demise of the market also signalled the end for the Goose Fair on that site, closing a chapter of history that stretched back for centuries.

The last Goose Fair in the market place was held in 1927, under the shadow of the new, partially built Council House. Goose Fair then moved to its current home on The Forest.

The market soon followed. The stalls were taken down for the final time and the cobblestones replaced by great slabs of stone, thus lending a fond nickname to the threequarters of a square mile of city space.

And looking down on the scene is Howitt's remarkable creation, topped by the impressive dome.

The view from the top of the dome, reached by a demanding climb of 70 steps, is worth the effort.

Standing 200ft above the city, it is decorated with sculptures representing Law, Prosperity, Knowledge and Commerce.

There are five bells weighing more than 16 tonnes, one of them (Little John), said to be the biggest of all tuned bells, alone weighs ten tonnes.

Except for the great Peter of York, it is the heaviest bell in the provinces, and the hammer for striking the hours on it, weighs a quarter of a tonne.

The dome looks down to the floor of a spacious arcade of shops and offices, approached by great arches from the streets. Round the bottom of the dome we read that the Corporation of Nottingham erected this building for Counsel and Welcome, and to show Merchandise and Crafts.

The spandrels of the dome are enriched with frescoes by a Nottingham artist, Noel Denholm Davis, showing in unfading colour, four scenes in the city's story: the coming of the Danes, the Conqueror ordering the building of the Castle, Robin Hood and his band, and Charles I raising his standard.

On the ground floor of the Council House front, looking down on the great square, an arcaded portico guarded by two lions, leads to the loggia.

Above the arcade are eight columns supporting a pediment with sculpture representing the activities of the city.

There are about 20 figures and a group of animals sculptured by Joseph Else, a one time principal of the College of Art.

In the middle is Justice with scales and a golden sword, her eyes open; Education and Law stand beside her; Labour has a team of horses, and Agriculture has sheep and oxen. Another group represents Motherhood.

The dining hall, Nottingham Council House.

The business of running the city of Nottingham.

A mason is erecting a column, a sculptor is carving figures of a woman and a child, there is an artist with his palette and a woman with musical instruments, and a reclining figure is bearing a model of the domed Council House.

Above the great windows of the reception hall, which look on to the square from behind the eight columns, runs a charming frieze with a procession of sturdy children engaged in the arts and crafts and industries in which Nottingham is, or has been, renowned.

There are reapers, weavers, spinners and iron workers with anvil and forge.

Eight children carry a great bell, reminding us of the bell founders famous here from the 16th to the 18th century; and eight little coal miners are hacking and drawing tubs of coal, reminding us of the days when such children worked in the mines.

Children working on the tomb of a knight recall the alabaster carvers famous in medieval centuries, and leather workers represent an industry that thrived in the city until recent times.

In the floor of the entrance hall is a mosaic of the city arms made up of 700 pieces. The balustraded staircase is lit by a beautiful dome of 144 panels of amber-tinted glass.

At the top of the first flight of steps stands William Reid Dick's bronze figure of a woman holding out her arms in welcome, above her a fine wall painting by Noel Denholm Davis, representing Merchandise, Counsel, Welcome and Crafts.

All the floors have panelled rooms with lovely ceilings and hidden lights, or light shining from beautiful electroliers of bronze or crystal. The woodwork is walnut and oak.

The reception hall has 20 fine columns and a panelled ceiling, decorated in cream relieved with pink and blue and gold.

Its floor is oak, walnut and pearwood and at one end is a mirrored wall adding to the charm, while looking down from above are galleries for minstrels and guests.

The Lord Mayor's parlour has on each side of the fireplace and the door, exquisite carvings in limewood of flowers, fruit and wheat, and some panelling from Aston Hall in Derbyshire.

The handsome dining hall has walnut walls with a striking figured panel over the fireplace, and the room of the lady mayoress is in Adam style with green and gold walls.

In the Members' Room the ceiling is enriched with vines, and on the table is the telephone which we are told was the 100,000th instrument installed in the north Midlands.

The Council Chamber forms a semi-circle, where every member sits within 26 feet of the Lord Mayor's chair.

The walls are panelled with walnut, with loose tapestry panels over a lining of seaweed, an ingenious device for helping the acoustics of the chamber.

One of the mottoes here is: "Laws are made for the good and safety of the State".

There is a small mallet (for the chairman's use) made of oak from a pier of old Trent Bridge, and there are pictures of old Nottingham by Thomas Hammond on the walls of the corridors.

Thus is completed the image of our principal building which has been the scene of memorable and joyous occasions ranging from royal visits to honouring successful city individuals and groups who have brought glory home to Nottingham.

Chapter Twenty-Four
King Tommy

JACKIE Sewell, who once carried the tag of England's most expensive footballer, insists there was no rivalry between him and his great mate Tommy Lawton when it came to scoring goals.

But with a broad grin he tells a wonderful story which suggests there was a touch of 'anything you can do...' when they played together.

Notts were playing, and thrashing, Newport County. Jackie, a sharp and nippy inside forward, had scored four goals to the mighty Lawton's three when he went to meet a cross which had goal written all over it.

"Next thing I know I've been knocked flying. I look up and the ball is in the corner of the net and Tommy is picking me up – after he had flattened me.

"I said 'what's going on Tom' and he replied 'I wasn't going to let you get another and beat me'!"

Notts won that match 11-1, honours even between Sewell and Lawton, four goals apiece.

That was in the season before the great promotion push. Jackie proudly points out that by the end of that campaign he had outscored Tommy 26 goals to 20. But he has no doubt Tommy was the catalyst that turned them into champions the following year.

Lawton had arrived in November '47 – a record £20,000 signing from First Division Chelsea.

Jackie, who had been at Meadow Lane since the age of 17, coming down from his home village of Kells on the north-west coast, remembers hearing the news that England's number one centre-forward was about to join the Magpies.

"We all sat in the dressing room and said 'oh yes, we believe that when we see it'."

But Notts manager Arthur Stollery was a pal of Tommy and persuaded him to drop down the divisions.

The effect he had on the city, the team and especially Jackie Sewell, was remarkable.

His first home game was against Bristol Rovers in front of 31,450 fans — 10,000 more than at any previous match that season.

Lawton scored two and Jackie, who had only four goals to his credit up to then, scored the other two.

Lawton got another two in the next game, then Jackie got a hat-trick... a wonderful partnership had been born.

Lawton on England duty against Holland – he scored four goals.

Tommy Lawton in action at Meadow Lane.

KING TOMMY

"Tommy said when he came, if we don't get promotion in two or three seasons, his house would have to go," said Jackie, who is not sure to this day if he was joking or not.

But it didn't matter. Come the 1949-50 season – "everything just clicked into place".

"We had a great bunch of blokes" – Jackie reels off the names without hesitation: Eddie Gannon, Frank Broome, Tommy Johnston, Tommy Deans, Harry Adamson, Bill Evans, Bill Baxter, Aubrey Southall, Roy Smith, Norman Rigby, Fred Evans – but Tommy was the leader.

"If you missed a chance he would give you a deadly stare. I watched the lad Cole miss a sitter for United – Tommy would have kicked him over the crossbar!

"Tommy used to organise these games, like head tennis, to get everyone heading the ball properly. Woebetide anyone who said they couldn't do it."

Tommy once said: "Stan Matthews was the greatest player that every went on to a football pitch. I used to play bloody hell with him if he crossed the ball and the laces were facing the wrong side."

But Jackie says it was all good fun that season.

"Tommy used to give me a nod or a wink and I would know just where to run for him to lay it off," he recalls.

They scored 50 league goals between them – Tommy 31, Jackie 20 – Notts

Lawton shakes hands with Field Marshall Montgomery before an England game.

Jackie Sewell.

lost only nine games and attracted huge crowds to Meadow Lane, topped by the 46,000 who turned up for the home game against Forest: 2-0 win with Jackie and Tommy the scorers.

But the most memorable day came in December when they met Forest at the City Ground for the first league clash since 1935.

In front of 37,000 fans Tommy gave Notts the lead with a header so ferocious those who saw it remember it to this day. Frank Broome's second half effort clinched a 2-1 victory.

By the end of the season Notts were champions by a stretch, finishing seven points ahead of Northampton, scoring a total of 95 goals along the way.

The return to Division Two began promisingly, with Notts signing Leon Leuty, but Tommy was struggling for goals – he finished the season with only nine – and in March came the bombshell.

Sewell, at that time the club's all-time leading scorer with 97, was leaving for Sheffield Wednesday.

By that time he and Tommy had become the best of pals – a friendship that would last until the day Tommy died in 1996 – and Jackie admits: "I did not want to go, I did not want to leave such a great bunch."

But in those days, transfers were sorted out between boards of directors and the record £34,500 fee from Wednesday was too much for Notts to refuse.

"It worried me, that fee, but I remember walking round the Meadow Lane pitch with Tommy and he told me 'just go up there and do what you do – score goals – and let them worry about the money'."

The fans were stunned by the transfer, one supporters club branch even calling for a boycott in protest.

But although Jackie loved his time at Notts, and still lives within a couple of miles of the ground, there is no doubt the move benefited his career.

He went on to win a Second Division championship medal with the Owls, a cup winners medal with Aston Villa and six England caps, playing alongside the likes of Stan Matthews, Billy Wright and Nat Lofthouse – the only centre-forward who Jackie believes got anywhere near the prowess of Tommy.

Lawton honed those skills as a kid with Burnley, heading a ball hanging on

Sewell turns after notching another goal for the Magpies.

laces from a girder. If you didn't head the ball properly– the coach hit you with a stick. Think on Mr Beckham!

Three seasons of schoolboy football brought 378 goals and the attention of Everton who paid £6,500 for him to replace the ageing Dixie Dean.

In the 1937-38 championship season, Lawton topped the national scoring charts and was ready to step up to international level.

In one of the many interviews he gave later in life, Tommy delighted in a story about England centre half Alf Young, the giant Huddersfield defender, who was lining up against him at Goodison one day. "Are you young Lawton?" he asked. "Aye I am," said Tommy.

"Well now, I'm just warning you. Now thee can go past and the bloody ball can go past, but thee and the ball are not going past together.

"I've heard that you can go a bit, and I believe that, but you are not as big as me and I'll be bloody sure to bring you down to my speed."

But Alf, and his contemporaries never did. Lawton scored 231 goals in 376 games at club level, 22 goals in 23 international games.

Bill Shankly, no less, believed that Tommy was the best centre forward ever to pull on a pair of football boots.

And Jackie Sewell had no doubt that he would have been just as good today.

"If Tommy was playing today, he would still be one of the top two or three strikers around – but I tell you what, I am not sure these lads today would have survived in my time."

The last word belongs to Tommy who said, in an interview shortly before his death: "With the old ball, it was 12oz over the odds before half-time and you had to keep heading it.

"The ball now, I'd make it talk, I would. Backspin, topspin, I'd put bloody cross-spin on it."

Chapter Twenty-Five
Clough's Other Half

ASK any Forest supporter to sum up the best years at the City Ground and the answer, predictably, will be 'the Clough years'.

But that is not strictly true – a more accurate reply should be the Clough and Taylor years.

Brian Clough was, without doubt, one of the best managers the Football League has ever seen, but he was never quite as effective without his alter ego at his side.

Forest's greatest achievements: promotion from Division Two, the Football League title, two European Cups, a European Super Cup, not to mention a sprinkling of domestic league cup wins, came in those heady days between 1977-82 when the partnership flourished.

As a duo they had everything – a grip on tactics, players, motivation. They came across like a good cop-bad cop team, Clough providing the no-nonsense steel while Taylor always had his tongue thrust firmly in his cheek.

It was Taylor who spotted the potential world-beaters others either did not rate or would not touch. He saw the genius lurking within the overweight frame of John Robertson, he reckoned he could turn a wayward striker named Kenny Burns into a world class defender, he discovered a carpet fitter named Garry Birtles playing in non-league football, and, even in their early Derby days, came up with the inspiration of grabbing ageing Dave Mackay as the man to lead the Rams to glory.

Peter Taylor would often say his happiest days were during those City Ground years. Not only because of what they achieved, but because it was at the club he had supported from a boy.

Peter Taylor was born in The Meadows in 1928 and long before a modest talent at goalkeepign became noticed, he was a regular at the City Ground, watching from the terraces.

Years later, before it all turned sour, he would describe finding success in his home city as 'utopia'.

Taylor won a place on the City Ground playing staff at the age of 16 but it was with Coventry City that he made his professional debut, in 1950, and over the next five seasons he was in and out of the first team, chalking up a total of 86 appearances.

But in the uncanny way fate has of dealing the definitive hand, Taylor found himself sold to Middlesbrough where he quickly struck up a friendship with the club's prolific young striker Brian Clough.

Hours were spent after games discussing football – the players, the tactics, the future.

Peter Taylor towards the end of his career.

Larry Lloyd and Archie Gemmill among the many mourners at Peter's funeral.

So it was perhaps not unexpected, even though their careers had gone separate ways, that Clough would call his old friend when he got the manager's job at Hartlepools United in 1965.

Taylor had no hesitation, even taking a wage cut of £17 a week – no small sum in those days – to join his friend at the Victoria Ground.

It was to be a good grounding. The two men had to do everything from painting the offices to organising the meagre finances. Hartlepools were in a better state when Clough and Taylor left for Derby County two years later.

In 1969, led on the field by Dave Mackay, Derby won the Division Two championship and the legend was beginning to take shape.

But the following year, Peter Taylor received the first warning of health problems to come when he suffered a mild heart attack. Like most things in his life, he took it in his stride and two years later Derby were champions of the old Division One for the first time in their history.

Players like Kevin Hector, Archie Gemmill, John O'Hare and John McGovern had become national stars and the long-term future for Derby looked bright.

European triumph was set to follow when Derby got through to the champions cup semi-final only to lose in controversial circumstances to Juventus.

Clough and Taylor were idolised in Derby to such an extent that even the players threatened to go on strike when the pair suddenly left in the wake of a row with chairman Sam Longson.

Throughout the following years at Forest, rumours of a return to the Baseball Ground persisted and the Derby fans never gave up hope that the sorcerer and his apprentice would go back – they later got half their wish but it only served to prove the adage that you should never retrace old steps. More on that later.

Following the Derby departure, Clough and Taylor moved to Brighton. Clough then endured 44 traumatic days at Leeds before Forest gave him a call.

Clough took over at the City Ground and a year later he was joined by Taylor. The partnership – described by John Robertson as better than Morecambe and Wise – was back in harness.

For five hazy, crazy and glorious years, Forest would be the talk of the football world.

Great players came and went: Peter Withe, Tony Woodcock, Viv Anderson, Trevor Francis to name but a few; and there was the odd, inevitable mistake – Justin Fashanu and Asa Hartford the names that immediately spring to mind. Peter Taylor spotted them all and was happy to accept the responsibility, good or bad.

And alongside the trophies, came the praise for a style of football that was refreshing, attractive and never negative. That probably pleased them more than anything else.

It was a thrilling roller-coaster ride and of course it had to end sometime, but it was still a surprise when it finally happened.

The year was 1982 and Forest were having their worst season since Clough had arrived. There was all manner of rumours flying around: a rift between the two, financial problems at the club, rows over tactics, team selection, worries over Brian Clough's health.

A happy team – Taylor and Clough during the Forest glory years.

Off to work – Clough and Taylor head for the Forest dug out.

Taylor had had enough and to the surprise of most people he announced he was retiring to his Widmerpool home.

"It cannot last forever. I hope people will remember us as pioneers of management – the first to show that two heads are better than one."

The greatest partnership in English football was over – but that was only the beginning of a new chapter in this remarkable story.

Within a few months Taylor announced his return to the game… as manager of Derby County.

If that revelation dismayed Brian Clough, it was nothing compared to the anger he felt towards his old buddy when Taylor signed John Robertson while Forest were still trying to get the Scot to agree new terms.

Clough never forgave Taylor and if they spoke again, it was through lawyers as their relationship became more and more bitter.

Taylor enjoyed a brief, turbulent, and largely unsuccessful time at Derby – an FA Cup win over Forest perhaps the highlight – and in 1984 he left the ailing Division One side. He then became a scout for Notts County and later Leicester City.

But he was certainly winding down his football career and in October of 1990 was coming to the end of a month-long holiday in Majorca when he died of a heart attack.

The tributes poured in: "He will be remembered for what he achieved," said ex-Forest trainer Jimmy Gordon; "a marvellous sense of humour" said Ian

Bowyer, "he contributed so many good things to the game," said Frank Clark; "he showed great faith in me and I can never repay that debt," said Garry Birtles.

Even in death, however, controversy haunted Peter Taylor. There was criticism of Forest when they failed to hold a minute's silence at the first home game after his death – a 3-1 win over Everton which chairman of the day Maurice Roworth said was the most fitting tribute to Taylor's memory.

His death left Brian Clough with the lasting regret that they had not been able to heal their rift, a fact he has referred to on more than one occasion since. Clough did however, attend his old pal's funeral.

Taylor deserved a better epitaph – one that recalled not only his achievements but the fact that he was recognised as a man of great humour, and first and foremost a strong family man.

The Clough-Taylor partnership is part of football's folklore, and particularly Forest's.

It would be asking too much to expect that we will ever seen the like again.

Chapter Twenty-Six
Bare Knuckle Days

WHEN they buried big Ben Caunt, in 1861, the funeral drew a bigger crowd than Lord Byron's.

Yet today the lion-hearted bare-knuckle champion is largely forgotten in the town and county he represented so valiantly.

His grave has been in a dilapidated and neglected state for many years, and his legend is constantly overshadowed by that of Bendigo, the man he fought on three separate, bloody occasions.

This forgotten hero is the same man who had a popular song called *Pride of Nottingham* written about him and, so serious researchers suggest, was further honoured when Londoners began calling the hour bell of Westminster, Big Ben.

Son of a local gamekeeper who worked for Lord Byron, Ben grew into a 15 stone giant of a man who learned to fight against local poachers.

He decided to earn his fortune with his fists and became a professional fighter, winning a few minor bouts and with them, something of a local reputation.

But it was eclipsed by the exploits of William 'Bendigo' Thompson, the Nottingham man who was vanquishing all challengers and was feared throughout the land.

Ben was jealous of Bendigo's reputation and for two years he taunted the Nottingham man into fighting him.

Finally, on July 21 1835, at Appleby House, Nottingham, the two met in the ring – Bendigo was smaller, but quick and cunning; Caunt a giant of a man with rippling muscles.

For more than 20 rounds, Caunt tried to use brute force to subdue his opponent, throwing Bendigo to the ground and falling across his stomach and throat.

Bendigo used his brain, continually dropping to one knee to halt Caunt's attacks while taunting him with insults.

In round 22, Caunt's composure cracked. He struck Bendigo who was seated on his second's knee and was promptly disqualified.

Caunt continued to win fights and increase his legend until Bendigo agreed a return match, £300 aside.

The fight followed a similar pattern with Caunt trying to crush Bendigo in a bear-hug while the Nottingham man poured more insults on his opponent.

At one point Caunt attempted to crack his skull on a corner stake while Bendigo replied with a kick.

But when Caunt attempted to strangle Bendigo with a ring rope, all hell broke loose as the Nottingham Lambs, a notorious gang of ruffians who followed Bendigo everywhere, charged in to save their fighter.

An artist's impression of the second meeting title fight between Bendigo and Ben Caunt.

Once order was restored, the fight was allowed to continue until the 75th round when Bendigo was disqualified for going down without a blow.

The Lambs were furious and Ben Caunt was saved from a severe beating by his own tough followers, escaping on a stolen horse while the two gangs fought.

Ben claimed the title of Champion of England and eventually sailed for America where he made a fortune giving exhibitions.

But in his absence, Bendigo fought 'Deaf' Jem Burke for the championship and was presented with the official belt before retiring from the sport.

Caunt returned to his homeland, determined to settle the issue with Bendy. It took five years to bring him back into the ring and at 1pm on September 9 1845, at Lillington Level, Oxford, around 10,000 people turned up for the decider.

In his book *Bare Fist Fighters*, Dick Johnson recalls an epic 93-round contest, quoting a reporter of the day: "It proved to be one of the most scandalous brawls in boxing history. Both men committed every known foul and invented a good many more. Frequently, Bendigo was tossed from the ring, Caunt trying to crash him on the ring stakes or across the ropes to break his back.

"Bendigo's Nottingham Lambs sought and attempted to bludgeon Caunt when within striking distance."

Perhaps inevitably, the fight ended in controversy with Caunt disqualified.

Ben took one more fight – a 60-round draw with his brother-in-law Nat Langham of Hinckley, before retiring to become landlord of a public house in London.

But tragedy followed him when his two children perished in a fire.

They are buried in Hucknall Torkard churchyard, alongside Ben, who died of pneumonia on September 10 1861, at the age of 46.

Bendigo, who turned to drink following the end of his fighting career, ended up in jail with a judge's words ringing in his ears: "Bendigo, when you are sober you are one of the nicest men in Nottingham, but when you are drunk you ain't!"

As he sat in a cell, enduring his 28th prison sentence, Bendigo found religion and upon his release he joined the Good Templars, a religious sect.

He left behind his Nottingham cronies to travel the country as a preacher, drawing vast crowds. On one notable occasion in Birmingham he was heckled so loudly by a gang of ruffians, he was forced to draw on his pugilistic skills to sort out the troublemakers before returning to his sermon.

Death came to Bendigo in 1880, after a fall at his home. A year later a memorial was set up in Nottingham Cemetery in the shape of a life-size lion with the inscription "In life always brave, fighting like a lion, in death like a lamb, tranquil in Zion".

Nottingham fighter Dick Hill lived only 30 years, but he left behind a legend of bravery and ferocity in the ring.

Born in Nottingham in 1807, Dick became a giant of a man after being put to work in the forge of blacksmith and fearsome fighter Dan Woodward.

He began to spar with young Dick and it soon became clear he had some grasp of the noble art, continuing his education at sparring sessions held in city pubs including The Butchers Arms and Foresters Arms.

At 18 he decided to become a professional fighter and had his first bout at Breaston – 64 rounds lasting more than two hours giving Dick victory.

He quickly followed up this success with more wins over local men until challengers began to run out.

But then came forward one Edward Johnson, known as the Irish Snob, to issue a challenge and the match was made at a staggering £540 a side with hundreds more laid in bets.

The two men met at Melton Mowbray on a sunny day in 1828 and, roared on by his Irish supporters, Johnson quickly gained the upper hand, drawing first blood and achieving the first knock down.

But the strength and power of Hill's punching damaged his opponent's ribs. Like a hunter smelling blood, Dick hammered away at the Irish Snob's body and after only 18 rounds the sponge was thrown in by Johnson's second.

Over the next few years Hill fought more than a dozen bloody battles, his last a defeat at Bagthorpe by Harry Jones after 69 rounds.

On April 7 1837, Dick lost the biggest fight of all, his death being recorded in Nottingham.

A contemporary of Dick's was Sam Turner, born in 1802 at Toll House Hill near the Market Place.

After schooling at Bluecoat, he learned the art of pugilism from Bill Broadhead, the father of the Nottingham School of fighters.

In his first bout, against Jack Bowkes of Radford, Sam took just eight minutes to vanquish his opponent.

Later opponents included colourful characters like Gypsy Welch, the Trent

Dick Hill ramrods Johnson, the 'Irish Snob' with a classic left.

Boatman and Young Winterflood, but none could live with Sam and, at the age of 28, his career looked to be over.

But a brawl in a Nottingham pub some ten years later would bring Sam back into action.

He had occasion to throw a young ruffian into the street – leading to a challenge to settle the issue like men.

Sam, now 38 and ring rusty, surprised everyone by accepting and when the fighters met, notables like Ben Caunt, Bendigo, local champion Patsy Clay and Bill Broadhead were at the ringside.

Despite giving away height, weight and 12 years to his young opponent, Sam was victorious.

Such was his reputation following the win, other fighters sought his help and he became a celebrated trainer for the likes of Bendigo and Caunt, Harry Paulson, Dick Hill, Cain and many more.

He lived in comfort until 1887, finally being counted out in Nottingham at the age of 85.

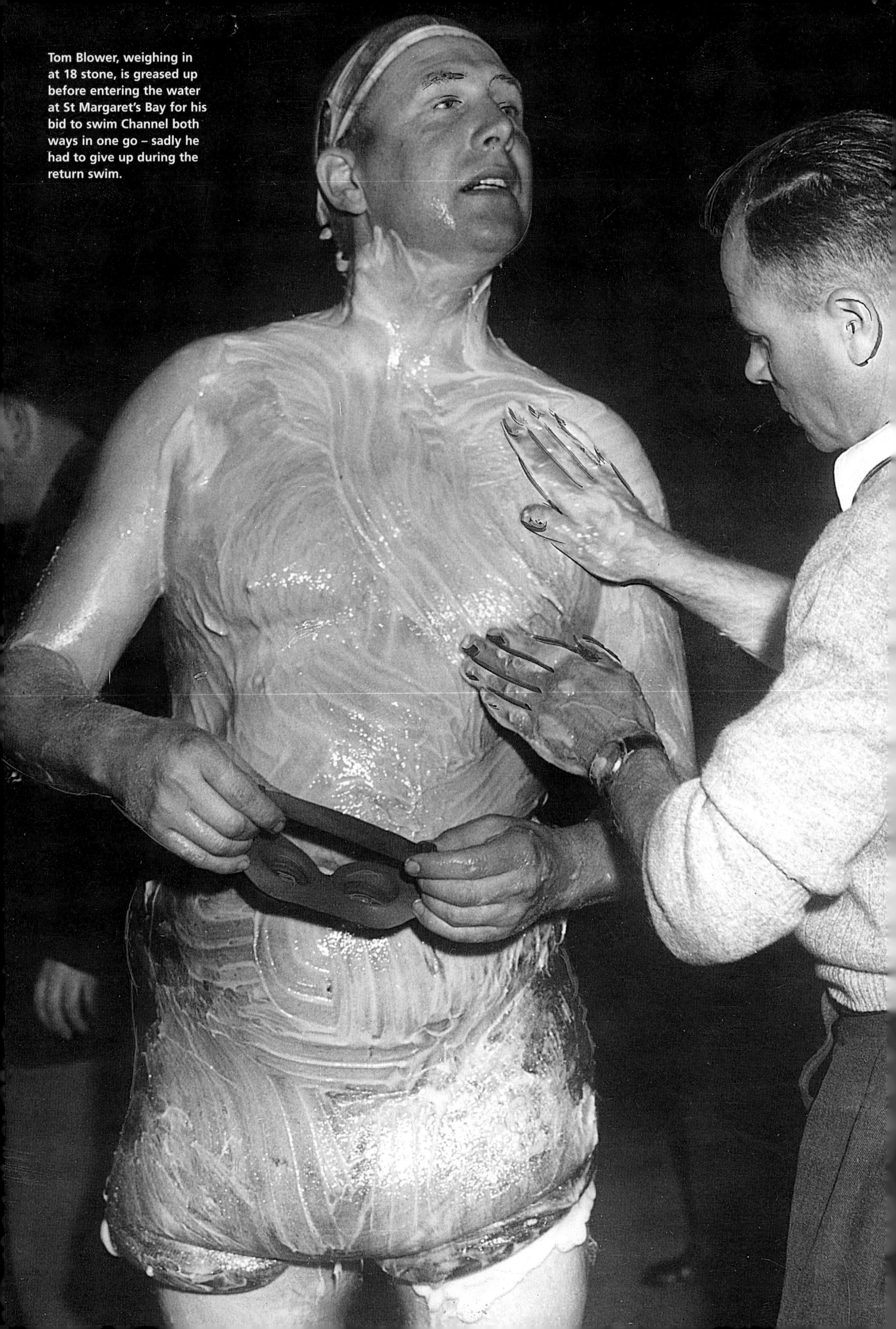

Tom Blower, weighing in at 18 stone, is greased up before entering the water at St Margaret's Bay for his bid to swim Channel both ways in one go – sadly he had to give up during the return swim.

Chapter Twenty-Seven
Torpedo Tom

NEARLY two stones overweight and his 6ft 5in body caked in 14lb of wool fat. In appearance, Tom Blower didn't conform to your average handsome athlete.

But Nottinghamshire's long distance swimmer is most certainly the stuff of which sporting legends are made.

"This is the strange side to distance swimming that stamps it as different from all other sports," Tom wrote in a series of articles for the local *Football News*. "Nobody is more delighted than my trainer 'Wag' Cragg when he knows that I am carrying surplus weight. He realises that the surplus body fat is only temporary; by the end of the swim it will be gone.

"Not only does the fat keep me from being chilled to the marrow but it also 'feeds' me during the swim."

When he penned that column in 1949, Tom Blower was at the height of his considerable fame. In 1935 he won the first of a series of Morecambe Cross Bay Championships, the first man outside Lancashire to win it.

Two years later, aged 23, 'Torpedo' Tom, as the media named him, swam the English Channel in a record 13 hours, 29 minutes.

In an era that saw men and women breach new barriers and reach out to new horizons, Tom Blower was a pioneering athlete who defied the worst a variety of cruel seas and rough waters could throw at him.

His inspirational achievements and tremendous feats of courage made the former Nottingham policeman nationwide news. As his fame spread, so he was feted throughout the land, always being accorded a civic reception at the Council House upon his return from another marathon effort.

Then, in July 1947, he dared to swim where no man had gone before, attempting to cross the icy waters of the Irish Channel.

At 9.53pm, with the light steadily fading, lion-hearted Tom slipped into the waters off Donaghadee on the coast of County Down.

Just over 25 miles of

Tom trains for another record-breaking attempt.

Tom is guest of honour at a civic reception. He is being toasted by the Lord Mayor Ald R. Shaw, left and Ald R.E. Ashworth, chairman of the Blower Swim Committee; Mr J.E. Powell, treasurer; and his trainer Mr C.E. Cragg.

some of the most treacherous waters and currents lay ahead. Bruised and battered he emerged from the waters at 1.19 the following afternoon at Port Challen Bay off the Galloway coast of Scotland.

As always, his devoted wife Clarice was first at his side – as she always had been throughout all his long distance swims, tucked under blankets and coats as temperatures dropped in the escort launch where she prepared his nourishing food and drink.

The public and media attention that followed was rather ironic.

An employee of tobacco giants John Player, Tom Blower was a rather shy, modest man, known for his humility by family and friends alike.

He worked tirelessly for boys' clubs in Notts and never forgot his roots in Dakin Street, Hyson Green, where he was born in 1914.

Ironically, the Berridge Road School pupil earned the nickname 'Carthorse' because he was so slow in short races.

He honed his swimming skills at Player's Athletic Club and swam solo marathons around the city's baths including one memorable 55?-mile swim at Victoria Baths which included 2,664 lengths, 39,600 strokes and the loss of a stone for Tom.

Tom also swam on the River Trent, being fed his favourite jam butties by Clarice as he literally came up for air and food beneath Trent Bridge.

He had traversed the Channel both ways. But his one remaining ambition was to swim it there and back – non-stop.

So it was on September 11 1951, that he set off from St Margaret's Bay, Kent, at 6am. Eighteen hours later he landed at Calais where he had a brief meal before beginning the return journey to England.

But dense fog had set in. Coupled with a relentless tide and pounding waves, it made Tom's task impossible. After three hours in the water he was forced to give up, his final fling against the elements ending in, by his own high standards, failure.

Tom promptly announced his retirement from long distance swimming.

Later that year he appeared on stage at the Royal Command Performance before quietly slipping into life as a sales representative with Player's, now living in Dartmouth with Clarice and their only son Mike.

While he conquered all before him at sea and was fearless amidst the most awesome and chilling waves, on land tragedy struck Tom Blower quickly and savagely.

On February 15 1955, aged just 41, he suffered a massive heart attack and died at his Dartmouth home.

Clarice, her eternal sweetheart cruelly snatched from her so young, was heartbroken. She lived out a lonely solitary existence before dying in obscurity in a Nottingham nursing home just a few years ago.

Son Mike emigrated to Canada and also died a young man, in his 40s, of a heart attack.

Today only a granddaughter remains as a living reminder of the Blower legend.

But Notts and the swimming fraternity have never forgotten Torpedo Tom.

Clarice's letters, unique photographs and certificates of honour are there for all to see at the city's Archive Office on Wilford Road.

Irish swimming associations regularly pay tribute to the great man and his granddaughter Ann, living in Colombia, Canada, possesses his dramatic and superb collection of silverware accumulated during his glittering career.

These days, sporting heroes are either wrapped in cotton wool or shirts which display their names. The least resistance to their pursuit of glory usually brings a tear, tantrum or two months on the treatment table.

For Tom Blower, who knew all about the loneliness of the long distance swimmer, adversity was an occupational hazard.

During his epic swim of the Irish Channel, he was battered and bruised by merciless waves. Cold, damp and in the darkness, he literally breathed salt water.

And when the tide turned against him, exhausted, he continued to stroke against all the odds. For four hours he swam without moving an inch forward before breaking through to complete his mission.

A mark of genuine sporting greatness. The stuff of which legends are truly made…

Life and Times…
Born: Nottingham 1914.
Learned to swim at seven as a Berridge Road School pupil.
Nicknamed "Carthorse" because he was so slow in short races.
1928: Won the Player's Athletic Club championships.

1935: Won the first of a series of Morecambe Cross Bay championship shields, the first man outside Lancashire to win it. Distance ten miles. In 1937 he was the only swimmer to finish in appalling conditions.

August 1937: At 23 he swam the Channel from Cap Gris Nez to Dover in 13 hours, 29 minutes, beating E. H. Temme's record set in 1934 by 23 minutes.

September 2 1939: the day before war broke out Tom won another Morecambe Cross Bay Shield.

1939: Joined the Royal Navy. Was awarded a bronze medal in April 1941 by the Humane Society for trying to rescue a drowning sailor.

July 1947: Swam the Irish Channel from Donaghadee, County Down, to Port Patrick in 15hr 26min. Until then, this treacherous and icy cold stretch of water had never been conquered by a swimmer.

May 1948: Swam non-stop for 30 hours in Victoria Baths, Sneinton (a distance of 55? miles) in preparation for his Channel attempt later that year. During the 2,664 lengths, 39,600 strokes marathon, Tom lost more than a stone.

August 1948: Tom went from Dover to Calais in 15? hours, joining a select band of men and women to have swum the Channel both ways.

August 1951: Given the Freedom of Nottingham baths.

September 1951: Made an unsuccessful attempt to swim Channel non-stop, both ways. He was in the water for 21 hours before being beaten by fog and strong tidal currents. Afterwards he announced that would be his last long distance swim.

February 17 1955: Died at his home in Britannia Avenue, Dartmouth, of a heart attack. Buried in Bulwell shortly afterwards.

Chapter Twenty-Eight
Your Evening Post

AT THE start of the 21st century, the *Nottingham Evening Post* is regarded by its tens of thousands of loyal readers as an essential part of their everyday lives.

They have many and varied reasons for reading what is recognised by the industry as one of the leading regional newspapers in the country – it has the awards to prove it.

From its unrivalled coverage of local news, to campaigns like Old and Cold, Silent Killer, Time for a Pint which have won praise from the highest levels of government, plus advertising pages for everything anyone's heart could desire, the *Post* sets out to be the newspaper for the people of its city and county.

In fact, it is upholding a tradition that was laid down more than 120 years ago. In 1878 to be precise.

An energetic Lincolnshire farmer named Thomas Forman was the man

The *Evening Post* building pictured around the turn of the century.

Thomas Forman.

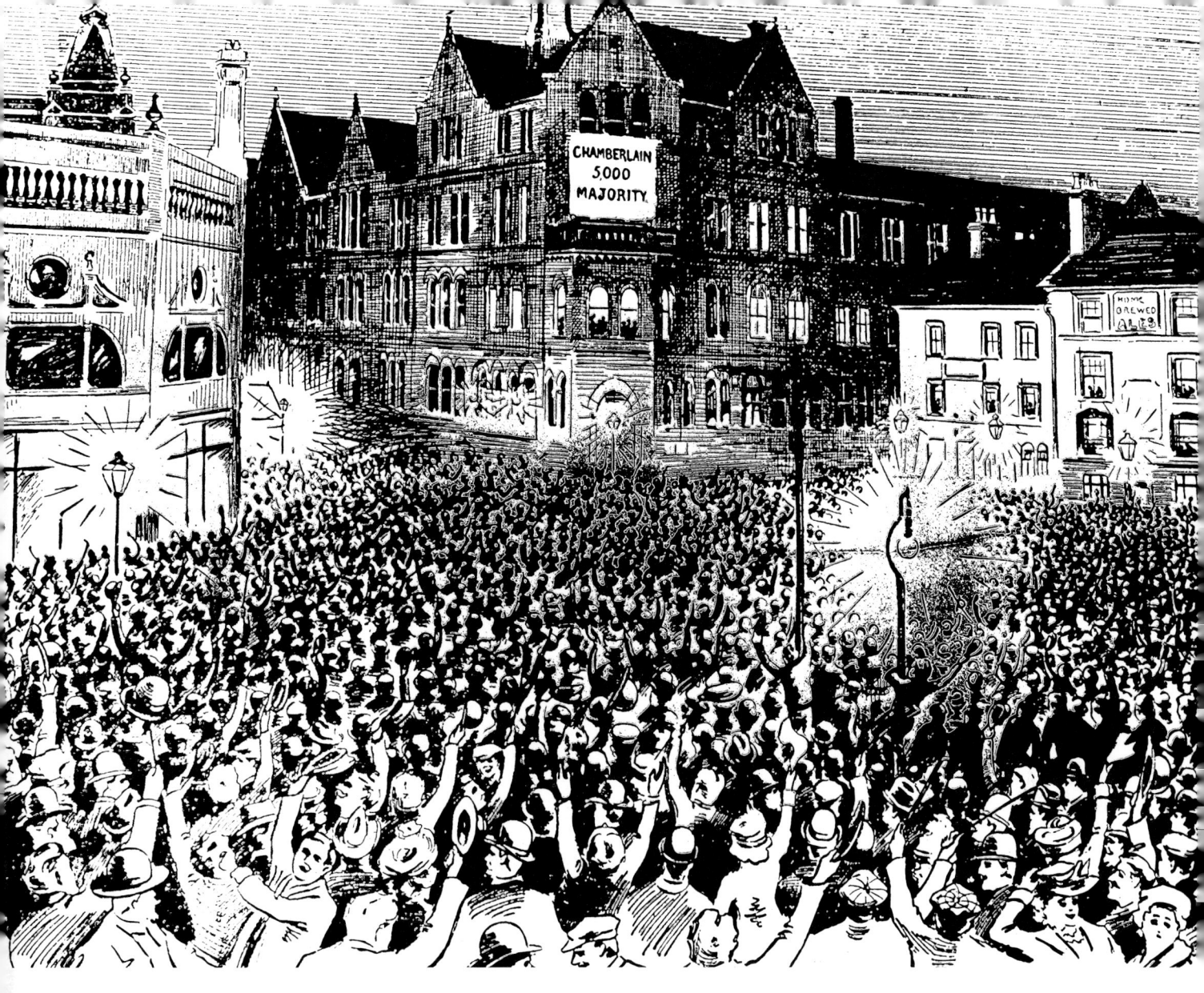

behind the newspaper. He had first bought a printing business in Long Row 30 years earlier and in 1861, taking advantage of Gladstone's relaxation of taxes on paper and advertisements, he brought out the *Daily Guardian*.

It was an instant success. Nottingham's citizens could not get enough of its mix of local, national and international news.

A weekly edition soon followed and by 1871 Thomas Forman's burgeoning empire had outgrown its Long Row premises and moved to a new site in Sherwood Street.

Thomas had been joined by his four sons, John, Arthur, Jesse and James when, in 1878 he decided to launch a sister paper to the morning *Daily Guardian*.

With the literary minded Jesse at the helm as editor, the first edition of the four-page *Evening Post* hit the streets at 3pm on Wednesday May 1 1878.

From the start it set out to be a news paper, promising to give in "as complete a form as can be obtained and at the earliest possible moment the intelligence of the day of issue."

The first edition covered stories about Zulu power in South Africa, a colliery strike in Bestwood, the opening of the Paris exhibition and a report of a 'shocking accident' in Sheffield in which a man was injured sliding down the banisters of a billiard saloon. The mind boggles!

An example of how the *Post* has always been at the heart of the news.

Compositors put together the pages of the *Post* in the pre-computer era.

These were pioneering days with the *Post* having to cope with primitive telephone communications and distribution by pony and cart. Although the box carts as they were called used to leave the building at breakneck speed, it took hours to get the papers delivered to regular subscribers and even longer by train to reach towns like Chesterfield, Derby, Loughborough and Lincoln which were all within the *Post*'s circulation area.

Horse and cart remained the primary means of transport until 1949 when the first *Post* van arrived, although a private car and a Railton Straight Eight lorry were used for distribution.

That first van was painted in navy blue and black. It was not until 1969 that the familiar blue and yellow livery was introduced.

It should be remembered, as we look at the ultra-fast, hugely expensive high-tech computer equipment used to produce the modern *Post*, that in the early, pioneering days, every word was set by hand in what was a dirty and laborious process.

The introduction of the Linotype machine around the time war broke out in

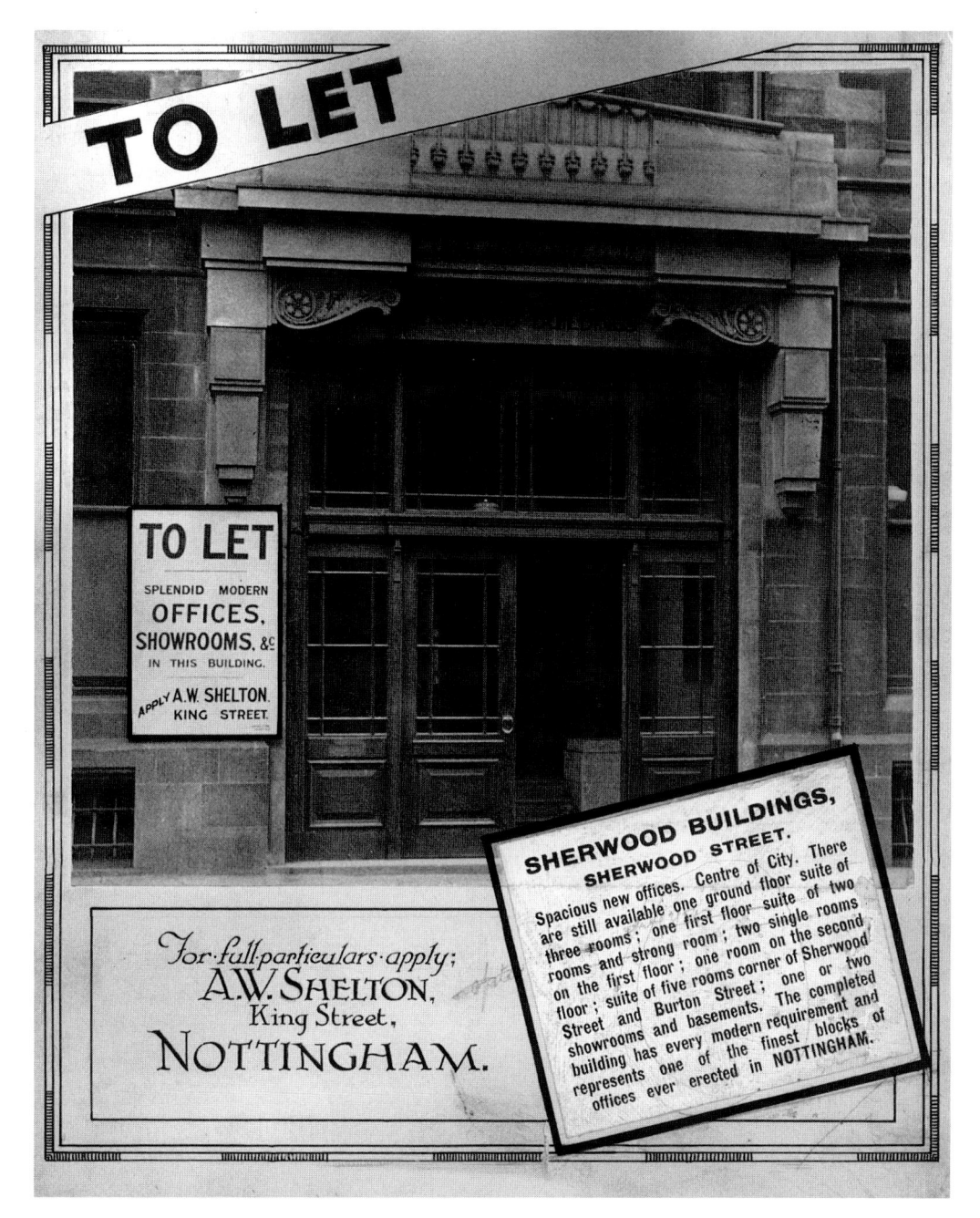

The offices in Sherwood Street which was home to the newspaper before it moved to Forman Street.

1914 brought a major step forward as a skilled operator sitting at a typewriter kind of keyboard was able to tap out a line of type in pretty quick time.

The skilled old handsetters probably looked on this new fangled machinery with something approaching disdain. They were still at work into the 1920s and could show a nifty turn of speed themselves.

The linotype machine ruled for 50 years until the onset of the computer age and, in keeping with its pioneering origins, the *Post* became, in 1967, the first newspaper in the United Kingdom to install a general purpose computer for setting editorial text and advertisements.

A year later the accounts department was computerised and by 1972 the high-tech revolution had also reach classified advertising.

In 1973, the *Evening Post* was being printed entirely by computerised photo-typesetting materials.

The award-winning *Post*'s proud new home at Castle Wharf.

Those advances have continued over the ensuing decades with ever more sophisticated systems being introduced to bring us to the modern newspaper with its full colour, multi-page editions.

It is a far cry from the newspaper launched by Thomas Forman and taken on down the line by Thomas Bailey Forman, Dorothea Forman Hardy, Thomas Eben Forman Hardy and finally his son Nicholas, the last member of the family to control the newspaper.

In the early 1990s, he made the decision to sell the *Post* to Northcliffe Newpapers. One Nottingham tradition had come to an end and, within 18 months another followed. The *Evening Post* quit its spiritual home in Forman Street for new, modern, purpose-built premises at Castle Wharf.

The outdated, Dickensian Forman Street building was demolished and redeveloped as the ultra-modern Cornerhouse cinema and entertainment complex.

A new chapter in Nottingham's newspaper history was being written.